THE MAN
THE NAZIS
COULDN'T
CATCH

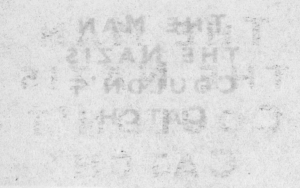

THE MAN
THE NAZIS
COULDN'T
CATCH

JOHN LAFFIN

SUTTON PUBLISHING

This book was first published in 1984 by
Sutton Publishing Limited · Phoenix Mill
Thrupp · Stroud · Gloucestershire · GL5 2BU

This new edition first published in 2004

British Library Cataloguing in Publication Data
A catalogue record for this book is available from the British
Library.

ISBN 0 7509 3547 2

Typeset in 12/13pt Joanna MT.
Typesetting and origination by
Sutton Publishing Limited.
Printed and bound in Great Britain by
J.H. Haynes & Co. Ltd, Sparkford.

CONTENTS

I

THE TRAP

Early one wintry Tuesday afternoon in December 1941 a tense confrontation took place in a little cottage in the village of Provin, near Lille, in northern France. Most of France, like the rest of Europe, was under Nazi occupation and the Lille region was feeling the cruelty of the grinding German jackboot.

A meeting had been arranged in the street-corner bungalow by its owner, Felicien Lemaire, a Frenchman approaching middle age. A Communist, Lemaire was well connected with the Resistance movement and he had a profound belief in his ability to judge character. He was pleased with himself that day because he had brought off a meeting that was important to him. For some weeks he had been in touch with a group of people who were arranging to help servicemen to return to England. At that time, apart from airmen who had been shot down, a few soldiers were still at large in northern France; they had evaded capture or had escaped from the Germans and were in hiding. The Resistance movement was as yet in its development stage and the escape lines were not well organised.

Lemaire, who had aspirations as a Resistance chief, had induced Private Leonard Arlington, a Londoner aged twenty-one, of the Middlesex Regiment, to meet the lifeline group which would help him return to England. This had been a difficult job because Len was convinced that the group was bogus and that Lemaire had fallen into a trap. Thinnish and tall, blue-eyed and blond, Len was an unusually quiet young man whose formal education was limited. But his natural common sense was boundless and he had a nose for danger. To Lemaire,

Len's suspicions were deeply offensive because they implied that he had been tricked. Being so much older than Arlington he considered himself incomparably wiser. He had been insisting for weeks that Len should meet the group; there could be no risk in going that far. Len had already several times slipped through the Germans' hands and was acquiring a Scarlet Pimpernel reputation; he did not want to hand himself to them on a plate. But Lemaire was so insistent that after much argument Len finally agreed to talk to his friends.

When he came to the bungalow on that December day he knew he was taking a great risk, though he hoped that in an emergency he could slip out of the back of the house and escape across the fields. He sat in the Lemaire family's small front room, looked through the chintz curtains and wondered if this was the end of his freedom. He did not feel particularly courageous in risking his life, just a little annoyed with himself for having allowed Lemaire to talk him into the meeting. Madame Lemaire was also apprehensive but she knew how stubborn her husband could be. She knew about his vanity, too; he was proud of having direct contact with such an important British group. Now he had even gone to rendezvous with them while Len waited in the house with her. As they sat in front of the small wood fire they glanced worriedly at each other.

Len started up when he saw a black Citroen with white sidewall tyres pull up in front of the bungalow. It was a menacing type of car, much used by the Gestapo. First to alight was Lemaire who deferentially held open the door while two women got out. Then came the driver, a tall, big and powerful looking man, wearing a good overcoat and a trilby. Feeling even more nervous, Len half expected a lorryload of German soldiers to arrive and surround the house but all remained quiet.

The small party came up the short path between the rose bushes, walking as casually as family visitors. The women entered first, then the man, who had to stoop to enter. Aged about forty, he was not only big but impressive and good-looking, fair-haired with broad, firm and manly features and a friendly enough expression. He took the chair which Lemaire offered him and twirling it in his fingers he carefully placed it against the doorpost as if to block escape. When he sat down his bulk seemed ominous to Len in that small room. The two women sat together on a small settee opposite Len. One, called Renée, was nondescript and had little to say throughout the interview. The other woman was of a type young Len Arlington had never before met and despite his tension – which he kept very much under control – he could hardly take his eyes off her. She looked, he thought, expensive – it was the only word for her appearance. She had jet black hair cut in a short bob with a fringe just above her alert, intelligent eyes which were a strange green colour. Her skin was white and smooth and she looked about thirty-two or thirty-three.

Dressed in an expensive fur coat she seemed remarkably feline, rather like a sleek but dangerous cat. Neither woman was introduced but the man announced himself. 'I'm Captain Jack Evans of the Canadian Army,' he said, 'and you are the lucky chap who is going back to England.' His tone was jovial.

Len had decided on sight that Evans was a German and he thought, 'Well, crikey, Felicien's done for – he's absolutely done for. There's no way out of this.' It was characteristic of him to think about the plight of others before his own problems.

Quite calmly, and with a laugh, he said to Evans, 'Hey, wait a minute, I'd like to know a bit more about your plan.'

About this time Madame Lemaire went into the kitchen and closed the door; she sensed danger and felt sick and knew that she was better out of the plot that was developing in front of her.

Captain Evans took Len's objection badly. 'I give the orders, young man!' he said in a thundering voice. 'And you will obey them or you'll be in trouble when you get back to England. Regard me as your commanding officer. You have to understand that I have not come all the way from England to be ordered about by just anybody.' He glanced at the two women, who nodded agreement.

'All right,' Evans went on in a more friendly tone, 'I suppose I can tell you a little about the operation. These ladies are Red Cross nurses and together we will take you to Carvin' – Carvin was a nearby village – 'where they will bandage you from head to foot. We have to pass you off as a badly injured patient whom we are taking to Calais. Once we reach Calais we drive to the beach from where we signal with a torch out to sea. A British submarine is waiting there and it will send in a small boat. A few more hours after that and you will be in England. It's as easy as that.' He gave Len a friendly smile.

The feline woman was even more encouraging. 'When we reach Carvin,' she said in a lilting, attractive voice, 'there is a lump sum of sixty thousand francs waiting for you. It's your bonus for escaping.'

Len Arlington was young and an ordinary soldier but he had grown up in a tough environment where survival was a sixth sense, and he had been four years in an infantry regiment where realism and not romance was the everyday fact of life. He saw many flaws in the story he had just been told. For a start, he was not worth the risk these people were taking, if they were genuine; the British army had no desperate need to regain the services of Private Arlington. He was certainly not worth the immense sum of sixty thousand francs. That was laughable. The Army would not pay its men a penny to escape; it was always made clear that it was a soldier's duty to escape if he could.

More than this, Captain Jack Evans did not ring true as an army officer. Len did not know much about Canadians but he reckoned them to be pretty much like their English counterparts – and no British officer would have threatened him as Evans had; and he would not have addressed him as 'young man'. A real British officer would not have shouted at him; he would have said with quiet, no-nonsense firmness, 'It's not your decision, lad, but mine. Now, this is what we will do. . . .'

On top of all these false notes there was the idiocy about signalling a British submarine from Calais beach. Everybody in northern France knew that Calais was sewn up so tightly by the Wehrmacht that even a cat could not have slipped through. The idea of somebody standing on Calais beach and flashing a torch to a British submarine was pure fantasy.

The escape group explained how difficult it was to acquire

petrol from illegal sources; they got it at half a litre a time from friendly miners in the Lille region coalfields. It was impossible to make unnecessary trips.

'Now,' said Captain Evans, standing up, 'we have wasted enough time. If you are ready we will move on to Carvin.' A real British officer would not have said *If you are ready*; he would have said, 'Let's go.'

'What, terday,' Len said, treating the suggestion as a joke and exaggerating his Cockney accent. 'I can't do that – I've brought nothing with me.' He had remained seated just to emphasise that he was in no hurry.

Lemaire looked anxiously from Len to Evans. He had not said a word, probably because he felt himself to be in the presence of a British officer with an air of command, but his eyes urged Len to agree to the deal. As a Resistance man with ambition to become a chief and a hero he knew his reputation would grow if he could bring off this escape.

Captain Evans made an obvious show of forcing himself to be patient; he even smiled. 'You won't need anything,' he told Len. 'We have everything that you might want.'

Len was apprehensive and wondered when the Lugers would be produced and aimed at him but he said firmly, 'No, I can't leave today. I must tell my friends that I'm leaving and say goodbye. Also I have a few loose ends to tie up but I won't need more than twenty-four hours. I could be waiting here for you tomorrow.'

With his eyes Evans threw the initiative to the feline woman. 'We can't come back for you,' she said, 'we shall not have enough petrol – we are low enough as it is.' Then her tone became more menacing. 'As Captain Evans has already warned you, if you refuse to obey your orders you will be listed as a deserter and I'm afraid it will be the firing squad for you; twelve bullets will be waiting for you.'

From a Red Cross nurse this was rather an odd threat. She had been speaking in French so Len assumed that her English was poor – and that too was just a trifle strange.

He shrugged off the warning. 'That's a risk I will just have to take.'

Captain Evans came in again. 'All right then, the day after tomorrow. That should give you enough time. You will be here without fail?'

'Of course!' said Len. 'You don't think I would miss a chance like this!' Then he added slyly: 'Sixty thousand francs – how much would that be in English pounds?'

The question was intended to show that he had taken the bait. The captain's answer confirmed Len's suspicion that he was not British. 'Quite a few, I should imagine,' he said. He should have known exactly how many pounds.

The three visitors were now relaxed and Len knew from their manner that they thought they had convinced him that they were genuine. They stood up and shook hands with Felicien Lemaire. As he parted from Arlington, Evans said: 'By the way, do you know an Alex Keiller, a Scotsman?'

'I've heard of him,' he said.

'Whatever you do, not a word to him about this,' Evans said with heavy emphasis. 'He's a stool pigeon for the Germans. Well, we'll see you about three p.m. on Thursday.' He was giving Len even more time than he had asked for. He added sternly. 'Be here for your own sake, otherwise it's the firing squad.'

Len nodded, his face as serious as it ought to be for a man threatened with such an awful death. As the party left, the feline woman caught Len's eyes and gave him a look that was a mixture of you-can-trust-me-soldier and you're-for-it-if-you-fail-me. Lemaire accompanied the visitors into the cold afternoon air and Madame Lemaire, hearing them go, came out of the kitchen, her eyes troubled. She nodded slowly to Len, indicating that she shared his distrust. They heard the Citroen take off noisily and Lemaire came hurrying back. He spoke for the first time.

'What happened?' he asked Len. He sounded puzzled and irritated. 'When they came in you went as white as a sheet. What frightened you?'

'They did,' Len said. 'And I'm frightened for you.' Then his tension exploded. 'Felicien, can't you see what they are? They're

Germans!' He was still not thinking of himself but of the safety of the Lemaire family. 'Don't you realise what you've brought down on yourself? These people are Gestapo agents. That was obvious the moment they entered the room.'

Lemaire was angry. 'So you won't keep your promise to be here on Thursday?'

'Not on your nelly!' Len said. 'No, of course I won't. I'm lucky to be still free – and this will have to be adieu. I won't be coming back here.'

Madame Lemaire said worridly. 'I didn't like the look of them either; that's why I shut myself up in the kitchen.'

Lemaire was now very angry. 'You didn't do the right thing, Leonard. You could have told them that you would not come back, rather than bring them all the way out here for nothing. What am I to tell them on Thursday?'

Len gave a deep groan at Lemaire's pig-headedness. 'Tell them nothing! Then they might just leave you in peace. If I had admitted that I wouldn't be here on Thursday that would have been the end of all of us. They were all armed and could have taken us prisoner at once.'

Evans had not arrested Len and the others on the spot for several good reasons. The neighbours would have noticed a family going out into a public street while being threatened with revolvers; this would have identified Evans as a German and his cover would be blown. Also, as Len knew, Evans hoped that in making his hasty farewells the English soldier might well lead the Gestapo to other evaders and escapers or to Resistance people. Lemaire would still believe nothing against the 'brave' group which was helping British fighting men to return to England and he was as angry with his wife as with Len. When Len left the house Lemaire was still worried about the embarrassment he would have to face on Thursday. If enemy agents were watching the bungalow they did not see Len depart. He could move as quickly and as unobtrusively as a fox and he took a track across the fields to Annoeullin. He had an urgent task – to convince a Resistance leader, René Saublin, that the dangerous Evans group had to be killed before they broke into every Resistance cell in the region. He passed on the particulars and a description. 'It's dead serious, René,' he said.

'I'll circulate the information to all the groups,' Saublin said. 'These three won't last long once the men know about them. They'll finish up in some grave in the woods.'

Len slept well despite his tense experience but Saublin woke him early to say that Alex Keiller had been caught in Allennes-les-Marais and that a French family had been arrested with him. Also, a French family in Libercourt had been caught with a British escaped prisoner – betrayed, it was said, by a man posing as a British doctor who had been accompanied by two Red Cross nurses.

That day Len took an incredible and courageous risk. He returned to Provin to warn Lemaire once again of his great danger and to urge him to burn all the incriminating papers in the house. Lemaire stubbornly refused to believe that Captain Evans was a Nazi plant but he did destroy all papers connected with the Resistance. ·

On the Thursday afternoon Captain Evans arrived punctually with his two women friends. Relaxed and smiling, they entered the little house where a desperately embarrassed Lemaire explained that the British soldier had not arrived. Captain Evans reacted quickly and covering the garden path in three strides he blew a whistle – and a platoon of German troops came pounding from their hiding place up the street.

The shocked Lemaire and his younger son, Ernest, aged seventeen, were arrested. An older son, luckily, was away with the French navy. Madame Lemaire was not harmed, apparently because the Gestapo did not consider her dangerous. Lemaire was interrogated and tortured but would reveal nothing. He and his son were taken to Belsen concentration camp, a place of unremitting horror. Here Ernest was executed in front of his father's eyes. With great fortitude, Lemaire endured four years of brutality in Belsen; he must have reproached himself many times for not heeding Len Arlington's insistent warnings about the bogus British agents. Weak with hunger and reduced to a child's weight, Lemaire was carried home on a stretcher after liberation. Not wanting to distress his wife even further, he never did reveal the manner of his son's death but it was disclosed by the historian of the Resistance, Colonel Rémy. Ernest had been beheaded.

Len Arlington had risked his own life to save Lemaire and he had succeeded in saving himself. He was not to know it at the time but 'Captain Jack Evans' was, in fact, one of the Abwehr's most successful agents, Sonderfuhrer Heinz Eckert. The feline woman was Mathilde-Lily Carré, a Resistance worker who had turned traitor; she became known, infamously, as 'the Cat.' Private soldier Arlington, armed with nothing more than shrewd sense and a knack for survival, had outwitted two of the Nazis' best brains. Others were not so fortunate; Mathilde Carré was responsible for the deaths of sixty-two Resistance workers and patriots.

The Resistance went hunting for Captain Evans and his friends and a fortnight after they had arrested Felicien Lemaire the Germans walked into an ambush. A German army escort was not far away and during the shooting Evans and the Cat escaped; the other woman, Renée, was wounded. The Gestapo propaganda machine made much of the incident. They announced through the Press that the German police had rescued a party of French patriots who had been attacked by terrorists. The affair had ended favourably as only one woman was injured and she was recovering in the military hospital in Lille. That afternoon two uniformed pro-German Vichy police arrived at the hospital to take a statement from the victim of the terrorists' ambush. A nurse showed them into Renée's ward and left them talking to the patient. Moments later four shots cracked through the wards and nurses went running towards the sound; they found Renée dead in her bed. The Resistance men who had posed as policemen had vanished.

In those hard days the Germans had laid down the ground rules – murder, torture, hostage-taking – and the Resistance was prepared to play the same ruthless game. At the very moment when Renée was being shot dead the Gestapo was once again torturing Felicien Lemaire, who bore his agony with a bravery that owed something to the murder of his son.

Captain Evans and the Cat knew that their life expectancy in the Lille district was limited; their cover had been blown and the Resistance had marked them for death. They moved to other areas of France to trap Allied agents, evaders and escapees. Len Arlington, the victor in the battle of wits and will, stayed on in the district. At the time when 'Evans' tried to trap him, Len, having escaped from the Germany Army, had been evading the exasperated Gestapo and German field police for eighteen months. He would go on doing so for another three years.

Len Arlington was the man the Nazis could not catch. He saw more armed German troops than any British soldier of the war; he was at large in occupied France longer than any other British soldier and it is likely that he had more narrow escapes from capture than any Allied agent or soldier; at times whole battalions of enemy troops were trying to catch him. Some of his experiences were unique. As 'Lee-on-ar' (the French pronunciation of his first name) he became a legend in the north of France and though he never received any official recognition from his own country, other nations decorated him.

I would nominate him as one of the toughest soldiers of the British Army. But then Len Arlington had been trained as a 'Diehard' in the Middlesex Regiment and imbued with a will to survive and win and, if the odds became overwhelming, with the determination to 'die hard'.

In that training, and in the rigours of an earlier life in a school for unwanted children, Len Arlington laid the foundation for an astonishing Resistance career.

NOTE

The Abwehr, the organisation for which Heinz Eckert (Captain Evans) worked, was the Nazi military police organisation. It had two main branches, the Feldgendarmerie and the Feldpolizie. The Feldgendarmerie, the uniformed section, were as conspicuous with their brass plates hanging on their chests as the British military police in the red caps. The Feldpolizie, to which Eckert belonged, were in plain clothes and their principal task was to arrest suspects.

The Gestapo were the Geheime Staatspolizei, the Secret State Police, and they wore plain clothes.

It is sometimes difficult to tell, in a particular case involving Nazi action against the Resistance, if the Gestapo or the Abwehr was responsible. For their victims the distinction was academic, though the Gestapo had the more sinister reputation.

The SS, often mentioned in this book, was the Schutzstaffeln. Originally the SS had been Hitler's uniformed bodyguard. It grew into a vast military organisation of infantry and armoured stormtroopers. Highly indoctrinated in Nazi ideology, they were the administrators of the concentration camps and they were responsible for most of the massacres in the occupied countries. By July 1944 500,000 men served in the SS, the greater part in the Waffen-SS, which was made up of volunteers from the occupied or satellite countries. The Resistance 'executed' most of the SS French and Belgian traitors who fell into their hands.

2

HARD TIMES

Len Arlington grew up in the grim environment of an institution known as the Bermondsey Guardians Home, a refuge and school for orphan boys and girls – and straight out of a Dickens novel. Strictly speaking, Len was not an orphan but as his mother had put him 'into care' at the age of six months he was virtually parentless. Neither he nor the others at the Bermondsey home were ever shown any love or consideration.

The Principal of the Home was a Mr Fords, 'Monkey' to the children because he was always eating peanuts. His pockets were freshly stuffed with them each day and the hungry children watched him put them into his mouth with drooling longing. He even ate nuts while marching the children the two miles to church every Sunday. Rain, snow or hot sunshine, the four-mile route march – four times each Sunday – could never be evaded.

In the 1930s no Welfare State existed, hence there was no social worker who might have spotted the more obvious deficiencies and barbarities of the Bermondsey Guardians Home.

In the autumn the boys risked broken limbs to climb out of the dormitory windows and down the ivy-covered walls to raid nearby apple orchards. This was no mere devilment; they really needed the apples.

Monkey was constantly on patrol, with a cane hidden up his sleeve, looking for victims. He seemed to get pleasure from thrashing his charges on the backside. Even being sent to his study on a legitimate errand, to acquire exercise books or pencils for a teacher for instance, did not protect a boy.

'Ho-ho! What have you been up to, eh?' Monkey would say, getting to his feet and, magician-like, producing the cane.

'Nothing, sir, really! The teacher sent me!'

'Well, of course he did! Don't answer back, boy! Bend over and touch your toes.'

Fords would deliver what he always called 'six of the best', and send the victim back to his class; even the most outraged teacher dared not risk his job by protesting to the Head about the barbarity of his behaviour. Len took his share of punishment.

Once, a night watchman reported seeing ghosts in the orchards. Monkey Fords, who did not believe in ghosts, had the orchard watched and Len was one of the raiders caught; the boys had dressed themselves in sheets as a form of ghostly disguise. Marched to the dreaded study they were punished once more with 'six of the best'.

Len's only real pleasure came from his membership of the school band, in which he blew the trumpet. He liked music and through it he managed to escape, at least mentally, from the humdrum routine of the school.

Life at the 'Guardians' taught Len Arlington a lot about the principle and practice of not being caught. He escaped from the Home at the age of fifteen by volunteering for a farming job at Leigh, Sussex. Here his day started at four in the morning when he had a quick cup of tea at his lodging in Woodhatch, Reigate, before cycling the six miles to the farm. He began work at 5 a.m. and during the summer months he finished at 10 p.m.; in winter he was lucky – he could knock off at 7 p.m. Sunday was a little less rigorous since there was no work to be done in the fields but the cows had to be milked and the stables cleaned out. His employer permitted him three 'free' hours each week. He had no need to worry about where to spend his annual holidays – there were no holidays. Len's pay was £1 a week; his landlady charged him 18 shillings (90p in modern currency) so he was left with 2s (10p) for himself. He had bought his bike for £1 2s down and 6d a week.

On Sundays in fine weather he cycled to the Royal Air Force station near Redhill where he watched Hawker Fury fighters

practising acrobatics. Interested in flying, Len intended to join
the RAF when he turned 18. He was a keen student of aircraft
speed, performance, design and armament. One day at the farm
Len was leaning on a fork watching the fascinating aerobatics
of an RAF Tiger Moth when his employer came by. 'You're
sacked for loafing on the job,' he said, in the manner of the day.
'Get off the farm.' Like annual holidays, notice of dismissal was
non-existent.

The RAF might later have had Len Arlington in its ranks if its
aeroplanes had not fascinated him so much; it was sad irony. He
was seventeen and a half, he had no home and he wanted
regular meals and a roof over his head. It was 1937, jobs were
scarce and to Len the Army seemed the only solution.

The day of his dismissal, he stood outside the barracks of the
Queen's Regiment in Guildford for more than an hour, trying
to work up the courage to enter. The statue-like stillness of the
sentry at the gate put him off. Then he saw a sergeant striding
along the pavement towards the gate, a magnificent figure in
his sharply-creased khaki trousers and well-fitting jacket,
complete with white belt and the red sash of Orderly Sergeant.
Tight-fitting puttees encased his legs, his boots sparkled as
though varnished and in his hand was a silver-headed cane.

Len jumped into his path, swallowed hard and blurted, 'I
want to join the army.'

'You're rather young,' the sergeant said, eyeing his smooth
skinned face. 'How old are you?'

'Seventeen and a half.'

'You're six months under age,' the sergeant said. 'Come back
when you're eighteen.' He patted Len paternally on the
shoulder and started through the gates.

'But sir!' Len bleated. 'I want to join the supplementary
reserve for six months. The enlisting age is seventeen and a half.
Then I'll be eighteen and can join the regulars.'

'Of course!' the sergeant said, turning smartly around.

'What was I thinking about! Yes, you can join the
supplementary reserve. Come along son, I'll take you to see the
recruiting sergeant.'

The recruiting sergeant arranged an on-the-spot medical examination. It was fairly perfunctory in 1937; any man who was not lame and not obviously suffering from tuberculosis, idiocy or venereal disease was accepted. After life in the Home and on the farm Len was fitter than most recruits so he was rapidly passed as A1. The sergeant swore him in, gave him his first day's pay – two shillings – and sent him off to the NAAFI (Navy, Army and Air Force Institute): that haven where soldiers could play billiards, buy a cup of char and a wad (tea and a bun) and escape from the drab routine of army life.

While Len was taking in the NAAFI surroundings he met an old friend from the 'Guardians', a youth named Freddie Fords, who was also joining the supplementary reserve. Both boys had the same idea – to see how they liked the army before committing themselves to it permanently. As army reservists, though, they would be liable to call-up if war broke out. That evening the two of them collected their railway warrants from the recruiting sergeant and travelled to Mill Hill, London, where they reported to Inglis Barracks, home of the Middlesex Regiment.

It was perhaps a case of God moving in mysterious ways. In seeing to it that Len was posted to this regiment rather than any other He was making sure that Len was being trained for a very tough life. The Middlesex Regiment won its nickname at the battle of Albuhera, Spain, in 1811. As the regiment stood in line on the ridge, exposed to fire from Napoleon's army, Colonel Inglis rode along the ranks saying, 'Die hard, men, die hard.' Being prepared to fight to the last and to die hard became the ruling principle of the regiment and it was drummed into all recruits. 'In this regiment,' they were told, 'we keep fighting even when we're down; we don't surrender and while there is a man left alive the regiment itself is alive.' They had proved it at Albuhera, when even the youngsters who played the fifes and drums stood steady under fire. 'You're not much use dead,' one instructor told Len, 'either to the regiment or to yourself, but if death is staring you in the face, lad, die hard. Understand? Fight hard, die hard. And as you die, take some of the bastards with you!' The 'Diehard' legend affected Len more than he knew at the time.

Len and a squad of other recruits were put through the timeless routine of filling in forms and being issued with a soldier's necessities, including the 'three biscuits' – soldier slang for the small horsehair mattresses which, when laid together, made a bed every bit as comfortable as the one at the 'Guardians'. A pint-size china mug, knife, fork and spoon, toothbrush and safety razor were part of the kit; Len, still beardless, had not much use for the razor. There were ribald comments when the recruits heard they were to get a 'housewife' – usually pronounced hussif – which turned out to be a small holdall containing needles, thread, darning wool and thimble.

After a late meal the recruits were marched to the gymnasium where a boxing tournament was in progress. As Len went in he passed a stretcher carrying away an unconscious, battered and very bloody soldier – one of the losers. For just this one occasion the latest recruits were spared the boxing ordeal but all the others were matched and, when their names were called, climbed into the ring for the institutionalised violence beloved by many commanding officers of the time. They used the regimental bouts to discover if they had a champion worthy of representing the regiment in Army contests.

That evening the most interesting fight was between a huge Irishman and a tall thin Geordie, both of whom had a healthy fear of the other. For the entire first round they pranced round each other without a blow being struck. The Regimental Sergeant Major, who was running the tournament, called both men to him and said sharply, 'This is supposed to be a boxing match, not a ballet dance. Now get back in there and let us see some real boxing.'

The Geordie took this as an order and suddenly landed a straight left on the Irishman's nose – and blood spurted. The stricken Irishman wiped his nose with the back of his glove, saw it was running red and went berserk. Arms flailing, he yelled, 'You bastard! You'll pay for that!'

Under a rain of swipes and punches the Geordie vaulted over the ropes and sprinted away, hotly pursued by the wild Irishman. The RSM was doubled up with laughter but Len couldn't see anything funny in the episode; what was in store for him, he wondered. But Army life was not really as tough as he had expected. Accustomed to getting up at 4 a.m., he found he had the luxury of lying in bed until 6.30 every morning. On Saturday, training finished at 12 noon and he had leave until Monday morning. On top of all this the food was good and plentiful.

The depot held a three-mile cross-country run and Len enjoyed it, expecially as he thought he had won. Nobody had overtaken him but to his surprise four other soldiers had reached the finishing line before him. They had shown soldierly initiative by boarding a London Transport bus but in their white gym shorts and vests they stood out all too boldly. They were seen by the Orderly Sergeant and charged. Their punishment was fourteen days confined to barracks ('jankers' to the army). This was a more severe punishment than might appear. Defaulters were plagued by bugle calls – 30 minutes before normal reveille, during tea-breaks, during the dinner hour; after 5.30 p.m. the call came every 30 minutes. On each occasion they had to double to the guardroom. When the last call came at 10 p.m. defaulters had to report in full marching order. Any infringement led to three days extra jankers. It was all very disagreeable.

Len had not yet fully realised that an army mess was rather different from the dining room at the school. At supper one evening he found himself contemplating the back of the bald head of a corporal at the next table. Coincidentally, Len had with him a ruler which he had been using at a map-reading lesson and with it he fired a small piece of tea-soaked bread at that inviting bald head. It was right on target. Len thought the corporal might be amused; instead, he jumped up and roared, 'Who threw that!' When nobody confessed he could only sit down, red-faced and angry.

Another recruit nudged Len and whispered, 'That was good. Let him have it again.'

Len, back in the spirit of the Home, did so, but this time the corporal swung round and caught the bread pellet full in the face. Next morning Len found himself the main character in an age-old army ritual – defaulters parade before the company commander. To his astonishment – he had been in the army less than two weeks – the magnificent RSM himself, the offended corporal and two escorts were also included in the performance. He was further surprised when the RSM snatched off his hat and threw it on the floor – the army's way of informing a soldier that he is about to face a charge. The hat comes off so that he cannot attack his company commander with it.

Len had no such desperate intention. He offered no excuse and was awarded eight days' CB He had blotted his army record.

At the end of March 1938 the passing-out parade was held; the men of the supplementary reserve had the choice of discharge or signing on for nine years as regulars. By individual interview the CO tried to persuade each of the roughly 100 recruits that the army was the best life a man could wish for. Only four, including Len Arlington, were convinced; the others had found it too tough; perhaps they were not prepared to 'die hard'. The four waited in trepidation for what the army would now do with them. The wait was brief. The very next morning a truck took them to Gosport, near Portsmouth, where the regiment itself was stationed. Here Len and his mates were posted to C Company and paraded before CSM Kennett, a vastly experienced middle-aged man who spoke to his new soldiers, to their astonishment, in quiet and civil tones. He even made them feel welcome. Then he shouted several times for Corporal Burt. 'Where the devil is that bloody corporal?' he said. 'He's never about when he's needed.'

Through an open barrack-room window a voice floated out. 'Natter, natter, natter. Just listen to that old windbag Kennett giving those new recruits the bull.'

Frozen, the recruits waited for the explosion. The CSM merely called, 'I'll come in there and do you, Private Knox.' And he grinned and winked at the newcomers.

A simulated female voice replied, 'Yes please Sergeant Major.'

CSM Kennett took it all as a joke. He had never been known to place a man on a charge; when he was angry he just used his tongue, softly or loudly according to the circumstances. The men respected him and he got good results from his recruits.

Once again, Len found that army life was not so hard. At six-thirty in the morning many soldiers made a dash for the cookhouse where a cup of strong, hot sweet tea was waiting. But tea was also available in bed; older soldiers who owned an electric kettle would brew up before reveille and sell a cup of tea to anybody who could pay one penny. For Len, brought up in the Guardians Home, this was unbelievable luxury.

While standing ready for his first instruction on a Vickers machine gun Len heard the Orderly Sergeant's stentorian voice. 'Private Arlington! Company commander's office at the double.'

Since nobody snatched off his hat this time Len was relieved to know he was not in trouble. It was just that his company commander had noticed from his records that he had won a cross-country race at the depot; would he like to join the battalion cross-country team? There were certain privileges – members of the team were excused all duties and they had running practice instead of the morning PT Len had no trouble in reaching an instant decision about joining the team. In a few weeks, with much healthy exercise along the sands of the Solent, he could run three miles in seventeen minutes.

For soldiers, there is always something to laugh at. One Saturday at Gosport the RSM held a parade and punished six men for not having their hair cut short in the regimental fashion. They were ordered to report to the parade ground at 4 p.m., hair properly cut, for a further inspection. The Orderly Sergeant ordered them to 'get fell in', then he expertly ran his eye over their uniforms. Satisfied, he reported to the RSM that the men were ready for inspection.

'Carry on, Sergeant,' the RSM ordered.

An unusually large number of men were watching this special parade and a hush now descended as the Orderly Sergeant gave the command, 'Remove headgear!' The six soldiers had done more than have their hair cut short; it had been completely removed and six bald heads glinted in the afternoon sunshine. A roar of laughter swept the parade ground.

The RSM could barely control his fury. 'March those men to the guardhouse, Sergeant!'

'On what charge, Sergeant Major?'

'Dumb insolence, you fool!' snapped the RSM.

The OC awarded each man fourteen days' CB but they agreed with the rest of the battalion that it was a small price to see the RSM's astonished anger.

Six hundred men took part in the brigade cross-country race and Len Arlington came in second.

When the battalion moved to Warminster, for a month under canvas, Len was posted to duties in the sergeant's mess but he kept up his cross-country training with three miles before breakfast. As he passed the officers' tents one morning he saw a remarkable sight – his Commanding Officer, Lieutenant-Colonel C.W. ('Wild Bill') Haydon, having an outdoor shower. Beside the colonel stood his batman with six buckets of cold water, which on command he threw over his CO while the colonel soaped himself. A tough Diehard, he had this daily outdoor cold-water shower throughout the year, regardless of the weather.

War against German was imminent – as Len found when he returned from his morning run one day. The battalion was rushed back to Gosport where the barracks were sandbagged. Officers delivered morale-raising lectures exhorting the soldiers to fight for king and country and, if taken prisoner, to 'give no comfort' to the enemy. But modern training was conspicuously lacking; the British Army of 1939 was a spit-and-polish organisation but it would soon be facing a new sort of dynamic, fast-moving and relentless army.

While working in the sergeants' mess, Len met Sergeant Michael Trotobas, a keen soldier of unusual background. Aged twenty-five, Trotobas had a French father and an Irish mother; having been brought up in France, he was bilingual – a fact which was to determine his wartime career as a Resistance leader. A champion boxer, runner and swimmer, Trotobas had joined the regiment in 1932 and was a soldier through and through; at that time he was in command of the battalion's machine-gun platoon. It did not then seem very likely that he would become one of the most daring of British agents in France during the Nazi occupation.

3

PHONY WAR

During August 1939 the war clouds became blacker. On August 21 the imminent conclusion of a Soviet-German pact was announced in Berlin to an astonished world. Hitler was determined to subjugate Poland and risk a larger war should Britain and France fulfil their treaty obligations to help Poland, but first he had to secure Russian neutrality.

On August 25 Britain confirmed its earlier guarantee to Poland. Appeals to Hitler from Roosevelt and Chamberlain, a papal peace broadcast and offers of mediation from Queen Wilhelmina of Holland and King Leopold of Belgium were followed by an eleventh-hour intervention from Mussolini.

On the south coast of England, Len Arlington, ever the interested spectator of military aircraft, saw the outdated Fairy Swordfish torpedo bombers on the way to their practice runs. With a speed of 125 mph and open cockpits, these 'stringbags' were years out of date. Fortunately, in reserve were the Hawker Hurricane and the Supermarine Spitfire.

The Middlesex men were given intensive rifle range practice. After a tiring day, Len's company commander, Captain Ferguson, sent back the motor transport and ordered the company to march the five miles to camp. The humane CSM Kennett protested but the CO had his way; the men voiced their feelings by singing the *Red Flag* all the way back to camp.

At dawn on Friday, September 1, German forces attacked Poland by land, sea and air. That same day in Britain general mobilisation was proclaimed, the next day the National Service Act was passed, introducing conscription, and on

September 3 Britain and France formally declared war on Germany.

The 2nd Battalion the Middlesex Regiment was to be part of the spearhead of the British Expeditionary Force and by mid-September was ready to move. As there would be no sergeants' mess in France Len Arlington was given the job of batman to Captain Porter, the transport officer, who had 300 vehicles under his command. This meant that Private Arlington would have the privilege of riding in the Captain's command truck, but that comfort was still to come. The regiment travelled by ferry to Cherbourg, then by train to Laval and finally by truck to northern France. Len did not quite know what to make of the French. On Cherbourg railway station he saw a father kissing his teenage son goodbye in public; Len had never known such personal affection and in any case such public emotion was un-British. On the long trip north he saw many French reservists on duty in their sky-blue un-military uniforms. They told the Tommies that their pay was a mere sou — a half-penny — a day and the generous Tommies loaded them with chocolates and cigarettes. This generosity was self-embarrassing so the soldiers made up for it by raiding the apple orchards.

When the British reached the famous battlefield names of World War I — Bapaume, Arras, Vimy Ridge — the French welcome became ecstatic. Len, the lad from London, who had never seen unchecked emotion, was overwhelmed by the excited French greetings — 'Hello Tommy! O.K. Tommy! Good Tommy!'

The battalion's billets were a disused cotton mill halfway between Gondecourt and Seclin and only twenty miles from the Belgian frontier. Captain Porter had a room in a small chateau, from where Len explored the countryside. It seemed that every second house in Gondecourt was a cafe, bistro or estaminet and they were always well patronised; it was possible to get drunk on two francs and this many British soldiers proceeded to do.

Outside the mill was the railway line, and at the base of the embankment the sanitary squads dug the battalion's latrines, around which they put canvas screens. But the latrines were in full view of the trains; the first one through, about seven a.m., was crowded with teenage girls who cheered the embarrassed Diehards.

A few days after arrival Len was leaving the cookhouse following an evening meal when the cook said, 'Look at that poor old devil, she must be starving.' He pointed to a woman in her eighties who was gathering the scraps the troops had thrown away and was putting them into an old bag. She wore the traditional wooden sabots and an ankle-length black dress. The cook shouted, ''Ere, Grandma! Don't eat that rubbish! Come over here and you can have a loaf.' He quickly made up a parcel containing a loaf of bread, some butter and cheese and handed it to Len. 'Run after her,' he said. 'Make her throw that garbage away and give her this.'

The old lady became alarmed and led Len at the run along the railway line and then took a path through garden allotments until she vanished into a cottage. Len hammered on the door and after a while it was opened by the frightened old lady who asked him in French, which he did not understand, 'What is it?'

He thrust the parcel into her hands, spotted the bag of chicken scraps and confiscated it. The garbage was not to be eaten, he explained, but the food he had given her was good, then he went outside and emptied the scraps into a chicken pen.

The puzzled old woman unwrapped her parcel in the kitchen, saw the army bounty, burst into laughter and spoke in rapid and excited French. 'They're a rum lot, these French,' Len told himself. The woman called shrilly and a tall, uniformed soldier came into the room. This was Desiré, her nephew, who in turn fetched the young daughter of the local schoolmaster who explained the situation in English. The old lady, Madame Estelle Ringot, was not a poor old peasant but a member of the family which owned the Cafe Ringot. Even so, she was always collecting scraps for her chickens and rabbits. Impressed by the Tommies' concern and kindness, Mme Ringot invited Len and the company cook for dinner that evening, a meal of eggs and chips with salad swamped in olive oil.

On this occasion Len met Mme Ringot's daughter-in-law, Zelfa, and her sons Edouard and Jean-Marie. It was Len's first contact with a French family and he enjoyed it. The French were hospitable and more open than British families Len had met; his own friendliness matched theirs and the Ringots and others took to him. Indeed, they took to the Tommies generally although an occasional brawl developed as a result of the hard drinking.

Zelfa Ringot lent Len a bicycle so that he could easily cover the three miles between Seclin and Gondecourt. Len was not the man to sit about the billets and one morning, having finished his duties for Captain Porter, he mounted the bike and happily set off for Gondecourt, reflecting on the strangeness of a war in which no fighting seemed to be taking place. He overtook a man of about sixty, jogging alone in running shorts and vest. Len had a ready affection for other runners in training and as he overtook the jogger he gave him a friendly and encouraging wink.

He cycled only a few yards when a terrific vocal explosion almost lifted him from the seat. '*That man there!*' It was the eternal voice of British military command though Len did not at first recognise it. 'Come here at once!'

Len was surprised by the man's good English and cycled back. 'What's the matter?' he asked sympathetically. 'Are you out of wind?'

The older man gave him a black scowl and roared, 'Don't you generally salute your commanding officer? Get off that bike and stand to attention!' It was Colonel Haydon and he really looked mad enough to justify his nickname of 'Wild Bill.' Len leapt off the bike, which collapsed beside him.

'What are you doing in Seclin? Why are you not on parade?' his colonel demanded.

'I am Captain Porter's batman, sir,' Len said in a conciliatory tone. 'I have just cleaned his billet and I am returning to the battalion in Gondecourt.'

'So you are Captain Porter's batman,' the colonel said sourly. 'Let me inform you that as from this moment your services as a batman will no longer be required by Captain Porter. You will be returning to the training company. Get yourself back to the battalion. And keep off that bicycle!'

Len gave a crisp salute and walked to Gondecourt, pushing the bike. His hopes that the CO might have forgotten the incident were dashed that evening when Captain Porter said, 'What trouble have you been in with the CO?'

Len's reply was the standard private soldier's answer. 'None sir.'

'You must have done something,' Porter said. 'His first words when he saw me in the mess this evening were "Porter, get rid of your batman, and send him back to a company." 'I'm afraid I can do nothing else.'

Next morning Len paraded with C Company. It was a bad time for private soldiers. A new RSM, named Peck, had decided that the battalion needed to be shaken up and his methods involved one drill parade after another. The mystified French saw the Diehards marching up and down Gondecourt's main street, marking time and forming fours; the British still marched in four ranks rather than the three which soon afterwards became universal. The French attitude was cynical; the magnificent drill might just stop the German assault infantry and armoured panzer divisions – for a few minutes. Meanwhile, the more human activities of the Tommies continued. Private Payne of Headquarter Company had become friendly with a French lady whose husband was serving on the Maginot Line. Friendship blossomed into intimacy, often given free rein in the lady's boudoir. One night the lovers were awakened by a furious banging on the front door and the lady looked out the window.

'Good God!' she said. 'It's my husband!'

She pushed Private Payne into the spare room and then ran downstairs to scold her husband for the racket he had been making. 'We have a British officer billeted with us,' she said. 'He sleeps in the spare room and you've probably woken him with your uproar.'

The French soldier accepted this story, enjoyed his week's leave and then vacated his place in the bed for Private Payne who took up where he had left off. Len Arlington was impressed with the lady's quick thinking; he had already noticed that the French got themselves into difficulties through lack of discretion – and that quick wits then often got them out of trouble.

A message came through in the middle of the night that the Germans were preparing to attack Belgium and within an hour the Diehards had gone northwards – leaving behind the love-exhausted Private Payne who had slept through the noise of 300 army trucks revving up not 200 yards from where his head lay next to that of his paramour. When he caught up with his unit in the Parc Barbieux near Roubaix he was awarded fourteen days' close arrest, which meant that he had an escort by his elbow night and day.

War might have been imminent but the presence of RSM Peck was more threatening. Equipment had to be spotlessly white under its coat of blanco and boots were highly polished; kerb stones in the park's lanes were whitewashed and above the ornamental archway at the entrance an enormous sign proclaimed 2ND BATTALION MIDDLESEX REGIMENT. Pleasure of practically every kind was severely curtailed and most of the 100 or so cafes were posted out of bounds as suspected brothels.

A brighter interlude occurred when it was announced that a General would visit the park. His staff car pulled up abruptly just short of the welcoming arch and Colonel Haydon doubled up and saluted as his men stood to attention on either side of the arch. It was not a happy occasion for the colonel. The angry general wanted to know what idiot was advertising the name of the regiment to the Germans and their sympathisers? That bloody sign would come down now. The chain of command went into action until the order reached the orderly sergeant who had ladders brought and the offending sign painted out. Only then did the general resume his inspection. As Haydon was not a popular officer the troops were pleased to see him roasted in public. But he was only one of many people who did not take the war seriously enough. For weeks, every day at eleven a.m., a German reconnaissance plane flew over the British front to take photographs and no British fighter was sent up to intercept it.

Len Arlington, who always had an eye and a nose for a way around obstacles, found a small nailed-up gate in the stockade-like wall of the park. Through this he and some comrades slipped each night for three weeks to head for the main boulevarde, where trams ran into Lille. On their return one evening Len, scouting ahead, found that the gate was slightly ajar, though he had left it tied up with string. His senses fogged with vin blanc, he investigated by getting down on his hands and knees, and with his nose almost on the ground he crawled around the gatepost. The night was dark but the shiny boots which his nose approached made their own light. Twisting his head Len let his eyes travel slowly upwards past the immaculate gaiters and the creased battledress trousers to the sergeant major's crown on the wrist.

'Good evening Sergeant Major,' he said affably to his own CSM Burns.

It was the beginning of a disciplinary action which led to extra guard duty for Len and his party, though the episode taught him further caution.

But caution deserted him when he was working with a squad at Lesquin, near Lille, unloading railway wagons. While lunching on bully beef sandwiches Len heard the sweet sounds of a harmonica – in fact almost heavenly sounds, as they were coming from the top of a brick stack, so tall that it seemed to be piercing the sky. It was being played by a Diehard sitting on the top of the chimney, his legs dangling in space. Without a thought, Len started to climb the rungs inside the chimney, going up quite rapidly, as a twenty-year-old soldier should do. A couple of hundred feet up he paused and looked down – and was stricken with a violent attack of vertigo. 'Crikey,' he said to himself, 'I'm done for now.' Slowly he started down the rungs, taking much longer to descend than to ascend. It was a sickening experience but it may have given Len the confidence he needed when slithering across dangerously sloping roofs to escape pursuing German army troops.

By now the French were calling the conflict le drôle de guerre – the queer war. Intelligence was certainly queer, because even

now the BEF was doing no serious combat training; apparently
the high command had still not realised that the new German
army was a formidable fighting machine. Following the
German invasion of Norway the battalion was paraded and the
adjutant handed it over to the CO; Colonel Haydon, upright
and immaculate, placed himself precisely before his command
and said loudly, 'Men, I have some bad news for you!'

He hesitated and the battalion waited for the worst. One of
his speeches was in itself bad news, some of the men thought.
The colonel went on, 'I shall be saying goodbye to the
Middlesex Regiment. I am leaving you to take command of the
British Expeditionary Force in Norway.'

The troops sent up a great cheer and the sergeants hurriedly
and frantically restored a form of order.

'I know that some of you will be glad to see me go,' Haydon
said, 'but if ever I need a good regiment I shall know where to
come for it.'

The men now began to boo. Haydon stood firm, smiling
broadly. The adjutant, who should have known better, stepped
forward and called, 'Now men, three cheers for our
commanding officer. Hip! Hip! Hip!'

The officers present gave a weak cheer but did not inspire the
other ranks to do so. The adjutant tried again, again without
response.

'Enough is enough, Major Reid,' Haydon said crisply,
'Dismiss the parade.'

He walked to his waiting car and the regiment saw him no
more. As a CO he was not as bad as the men had come to believe
but he lacked the common touch. Two years later, on June 1,
1942, he was commanding 150 Brigade near El Alamein, North
Africa, when Rommel's Africa Corps overran his headquarters.
Armed only with a swagger stick Haydon laid about the
Germans until he was shot dead. It was an impressive display of
courage if not of common sense; had he been armed with a
Tommy gun he might have taken some of the enemy with him.
But as a Diehard he had shown that he knew how to die.

Major Reid took over as Acting CO. Early on May 10 a

sergeant burst into the billets which Len was sharing with
others and shouted, 'Right lads, let's have you! The balloon's
gone up and this is it! Hitler has attacked Belgium. Get your
gear ready. We move in an hour.'

The 300 vehicles headed rapidly for the frontier at Baisieux
where the war was still so queer that the Belgian customs men
would not raise the barrier; even more queerly, the British
regiment waited eight hours for it to be lifted. Perhaps Colonel
Haydon would have smashed through it.

Even across the border the Middlesex – now under Lieut-Col.
B.G. Horrocks* – did not at first find the war; people were
relaxed and strolling in the streets, farmers were milking their
cows by the roadside and the trains were still running. As the
battalion entered Louvain a dozen old Heinkel biplanes shot up
the column without causing casualties but Louvain itself had
suffered; houses were on fire, the roads were bomb-cratered
and electric power lines were down.

About midnight the Diehards took up positions along a canal
bank. Len Arlington was awakened about 5 a.m. by strafing
Heinkels and Messerschmidts which made several unopposed
runs against British positions. Len, enthralled by the spectacle
in the early morning sun, tried to pot the incoming planes with
his .303 Lee Enfield. Then a violent blow on the jaw felled him
and he looked up from the ground to see a much older soldier,
named Smith, blubbering with fright. 'You bloody fool!' Smith
shouted. 'Don't stand there looking up at them! Don't you
know that your face shows white against the background? If
they see our position we've had it.'

Smith knew what he was talking about but Len was
aggrieved. 'Belt up grandad!' he snarled. 'Have a crap. You look
as if you need one.' And in defiance he let off a couple more
futile shots against the low-flying Messerschmidts.

---

* Later Lieut.-Gen. Sir Brian Horrocks, one of the most famous of British
Commanders.

The troops wondered when the RAF would appear, and about midday a Westland Lysander, an Army co-operation plane, came into sight. For the first time the British ack-ack gunners opened up – at the Lysander. Len, who knew his aircraft, was furious. 'The bastards! Can't they see it's one of ours?'

The pilot tried to get below the bursting shells but his plane suffered a direct hit, burst into flames and crashed. Then a dozen Messerschmidt 109s appeared – but were not challenged by the AA gunners. Nine enemy aircraft were apparently too many to take on. Len nearly wept with frustration.

Len's platoon commander, Lieut. Peters, called for volunteers to flush out any German parachutists in the area and Len – to get out of trench digging – was one who volunteered. They found that homes in the immediate vicinity had been evacuated; some had been abandoned so abruptly that radios were still playing. Peters found the door of one house open, heard sounds upstairs and, revolver in hand, cautiously climbed the stairs. As he dashed across the landing a shot rang out and a bullet crashed into the ceiling.

'You blasted idiot!' an angry voice called. 'Hold it everybody, we're coming out.'

A Guards captain, smoking pistol in hand, and two guardsmen came out of the room. 'Dammit all, sir,' said an offended Peters. 'You shot at me!'

'I should think so, the way you came charging in here!' the captain retorted. 'You're mightly lucky that bullet didn't blow your brains out. You should know better than to rush in like that without challenging first.'

German shells started to fall and the group found themselves, for the first time, under heavy fire. Rejoining the platoon they took up new positions on the edge of an orchard. Some local farmworkers who had been told to get away to safety came to offer a deal: if the Tommies would feed the animals they could have the eggs and milk. Len was the only man who knew how to milk so he became that platoon supplier of farm products; he even found fresh bread in the cellar.

The men settled down to sleep, only to be disturbed after

midnight by the noise of heavy vehicles manoeuvring on the
other side of the orchard. After blessed quiet for an hour the
infantrymen were again awakened by a flurry of shouted
commands, culminating in the bellowed order, 'Fire!' And a
battery of four 25-pounder guns opened up on German
positions. The shaken infantrymen found the racket unbearable
but after thirty minutes or so the bombardment ceased and they
heard the guns being limbered up. The battery made its creaking
way from the orchard and the Diehards settled down to an
exhausted sleep. A few minutes later German artillery retaliated
and shells began to explode around them. They spent the rest of
the night in slit trenches; it was not the last time that infantry
cursed the gunners for drawing a hornets' nest around their ears.

That afternoon another Lysander did brief battle against 20
Heinkels and 30 Messerschmidts before the gallant pilot met
his inevitable end. Len's platoon was pulled out of the farm to
join the rest of the company and on the way was halted by an
officer who came running down the road. 'Mount the Vickers
machine guns in the ditch facing the fields!' he ordered
urgently. A column of infantry had been sighted on the road
parallel to that taken by the British and was a prime target.

The range-finder, peering through his instrument, said
excitedly, 'Crikey! There's thousands of the bastards! Here, Len,
have a look.'

Len peered, saw an officer on horseback leading the column,
stared more closely into the glass and jumped up shouting, 'For
God's sake don't shoot! They're French troops!'

His warning came too late. One gun had begun to chatter
and the troops on the road scattered wildly. Soon a rifle was
raised with a white handkerchief attached and unseen hands
waved it furiously. A British officer went forward and found
that the troops were indeed allies, though Belgian, not French
as Len had supposed. Fortunately, the British gun had been
firing too high to cause casualties though the Belgians were
understandably indignant.

The Middlesex men moved into a forest, east of Louvain,
where they were kept in reserve. That night Len was on guard

patrolling the forest tracks, his turn for duty being between midnight and two a.m., a tense and testing time for soldiers fresh into action. At one o'clock he heard a rustling in the undergrowth and his skin prickled in alarm. Safety catch off and bullet in the chamber, Len called croakily, 'Halt! Who goes there?'

No answer came but the rustling continued and Len fired at the sound. At once there was a bellow, 'Friend! Don't shoot! It's me!' And the platoon sergeant exploded from the bushes. 'What's the game? Are you trying to murder me?'

'I was only following your orders, sergeant,' Len said. 'Challenge once, then fire.'

The sergeant, who had been answering the call of nature, had not heard the challenge but admitted, reluctantly, that he had only himself to blame for the near miss.

4

INTO BATTLE

Early next morning the troops for the first time saw the notorious Stuka 187 dive-bombers in action. Flying in line astern, four of the monoplanes, with their low, curved wings and fixed undercarriages, came swooping over a village like birds of prey. Their quarry was a passenger train, moving slowly like some giant and helpless caterpillar. The aircraft seemed to hover before they began a slow drop. Then their drop became a vicious dive with engines at full pitch and their sirens screeching their fearsome threat. Many a trained soldier found it difficult to stand his ground under the Stuka's noisy attack. The four planes came down almost vertically and released their bombs, scoring several direct hits on the helpless train. Passengers began to spill out and run as the aircraft zoomed higher before the pilots made strafing runs, machine-gunning the fleeing survivors. Len Arlington watched all this in horror and dejection, praying silently and vainly for the RAF or the French air force to put in an appearance.

That evening his battalion was rushed forward to counter-attack a village which the Germans had captured. The Tommies went in quickly and silently until the sergeant called 'Down lads!' Len shot into a doorway, snapped a round at a running German and missed and moments later saw a German helmet silhouetted above the shallow wall of a bridge. As he took aim the German rose fully to throw a grenade and Len's bullet hit him in the chest. But German casualties were light. The British troops had no grenades and some muttered sourly that the army should at least have given them some tins of boot polish or cakes of blanco to throw at the Germans.

The Middlesex men were withdrawn as rapidly as they had been rushed forward and back among trees they camouflaged their positions. The refugees had no such skill and no such opportunity; with the dawn the troops saw floods of people on the roads leading out of the battle area, women with babies in their arms, older men on carthorses, even a few people pushing their goods in wheelbarrows. Many carried all their possessions on their backs, wrapped in blankets or an eiderdown. Many of the coverings were a bright red and they seemed to attract the attention of German pilots. The resulting attacks convinced the panic-stricken people that the red blankets among them were carried by Fifth Columnists. Denounced to the nearest soldiers or gendarmes, many unfortunate people with red blankets were shot as spies.

Rumours also spread that German parachutists were dressed as nuns and this led to many an innocent refugee nun being roughly searched.

From where he stood Len saw a black saloon car which had broken down under its weight of luggage; the civilian driver was poking into the engine desperately trying to revive the dead vehicle. Some of the stream of refugees were threatening him for blocking the road. From a mile off, the watching Tommies saw Stuka dive-bombers getting ready for a strafing run – and in they came with sirens screaming to machine-gun and bomb the helpless Belgians, who scattered for what little cover they could find. The Germans kept up their attack for ten minutes and bodies littered the road. Len had already started running towards the scene and survivors were rushing back to the road to tend the wounded and cover the dead. He came upon a woman kneeling besides a small mound covered with a blanket; tears streamed down her face and her hands were clasped in prayer, but she held them out to Len when she saw his British uniform. 'My two children!' she said. 'They have killed my two children! Why?'

Helplessly, Len patted her hands and head. Further up the road the saloon car stood abandoned, its owner probably dead, and two dead horses lay in a ditch. People carried the casualties off the road. Len felt a terrible sense of guilt as if he personally had been responsible for the death of the two children. After a while he walked up the road, rounded a bend and sat on an upturned cart to survey the dismal scene while he inwardly raged at the Germans. In the distance he saw a dozen German planes swooping on some unseen target and realised that he was in a difficult position. His was the only uniform in sight but to a German pilot it might be excuse enough to strafe the line of refugees as a 'military column' – if he needed an excuse. In any case, enemy troops might soon appear. He walked away quickly, past the mother of the dead children, still on her knees praying. Then an astonishing spectacle met his eyes. A group of laughing civilians were busy with huge knives, carving up the dead horse and throwing great chunks into enamel basins. He knew that horseflesh was a delicacy in Belgium and France but the butchery, so soon after the air attack, was almost shocking.

As he returned to his own position German rifles cracked but Len reached safety – to find his sergeant furious. 'Where the hell do you think you've been?' he said, more as a reprimand than a question. Len could hardly say that his humanity had drawn him to the suffering Belgians; he just looked at the sergeant and shrugged his shoulders. 'Look through that range-finder and tell me what you see,' the NCO ordered.

Through the magnifying eye-piece Len recognised the road he had just left and beyond the road, in a field, a group of German soldiers around a machine gun. 'You see that!' the sergeant snapped. 'Well, we couldn't use our guns because we didn't want to run the risk of hitting you! Now get back to your position while we give those bastards a little of their own medicine.'

The British machine guns opened up. Their long bursts of fire hit the target but other German machine guns quickly retaliated and a hail of bullets ripped through the woods. A thirty-minute artillery bombardment followed, but the Middlesex men suffered no casualties. It was obvious to all of them, though, that the British were heavily outnumbered in tanks, planes, men and firepower, and that night they had a sample of German tactics. Planes droned over the woods and seconds later parachute flares lit up the woods as if with bright sunshine. Some men tried to extinguish the flares while others ran about aimlessly and blazed away at nothing in particular. Most of the men were convinced that an entire German parachute regiment was attacking them. Lieutenant Peters came running up to his platoon shouting, 'Stop that firing! The next man who fires a rifle without orders will be court-martialled!'

At daybreak the Middlesex men moved out on the first of many steps backwards towards the border, France and the beaches of Dunkirk. Len's platoon reached a deserted farmhouse, where they needed no urging to dig slit trenches. Then a few men, including Len, found a small barrel full of an orange liquid in a cellar. They tasted it – British soldiers will taste anything – found it delicious and took it to the sergeant.

'You can't drink that,' he said at once. 'Suppose it has been poisoned and left behind on purpose, just for muggins like you?' Still, he dipped a finger and tasted the orange liquid. 'Pity though, it tastes bloody good.' Then he shook his head. 'No, there's no way of knowing if it's okay. We can't take the risk.'

The soldier who was taking the barrel back to the cellar was passing through the farmyard when he shouted, 'Eh, you blokes! There's a cockerel here!'

'What about it?' the sergeant said. 'Never seen a cockerel before?'

'I mean what about catching it and trying this stuff on it.'

'Good thinking, lad,' the sergeant said.

Whooping soldiers corner the squawking bird and while the sergeant prised open its beak Len poured a tumbler of liquid down its throat and shut it in a coop. Twenty minutes later when he opened the door the cockerel staggered out, tried to flap its wings and fell flat on its back. There was a hush – then the bird struggled to its feet and lurched around the yard.

'The bird's alive so the stuff's okay,' the sergeant said, and solemnly he poured each man a small tumblerful of the precious hooch. Len never did know what it was.

Next morning the British were on the move again, ever backwards, while the German planes strafed every road.

Soldiers, civilians and horses perished by the way and mounds of quickly dug graves marked their passing. French engineers blew up a bridge just after Len's company crossed it and great chunks of stone and cement crashed around them.

'La guerre est fini!' excited and despairing villagers shouted to the troops aboard their trucks.

'They're off their bleedin' rockers,' Len told his mates. 'We haven't started to fight yet.' And when they heard that the Grenadier Guards had counter-attacked it did seem that the French opinion was premature.

But, like all soldiers close to battle, they did not hear much. They did not know, for instance, that the Belgian Army had lost 7,550 men killed and 15,850 wounded, though, on May 27, they did hear the result of this loss – King Leopold of Belgium had signed a separate peace agreement with the Nazis. The elimination of the Belgians opened a twenty-mile gap on the left flank of the BEF-French pocket, which was closed after fierce fighting.

The Middlesex men had been withdrawn to Wattrelos, near Roubaix, where they established positions in houses and farm buildings. About mid-morning A French civilian wearing overalls and a beret arrived outside the house where the Middlesex machine guns had been placed and with buckets of water and a broom he washed down the pavement in front of the house. A few minutes later two Messerschmidt fighters circled the town and swooped in on a strafing run, their bullets and cannon shells whanging against the walls of the house.

Nobody was wounded but Lieutenant Peters said suspiciously 'I wonder what made them single out this house in a whole town.' He spotted the pavement-washing Frenchman, who had taken cover, ordered the sergeant to bring him in, and sent for Platoon Sergeant Major Michael Trotobas. With his fluent French, Trotobas found out that the man was no spy but a good neighbour who washed the pavement every Saturday morning. With the spy scare at its height the Frenchman was lucky not to have been shot.

To relax, Len sat on the pavement and cleaned his rifle while three boys no older than eight stopped to watch him. By now proficient in patois, Len struck up a conversation and produced some chocolate he had pilfered in Belgium, which he shared among them. 'Now buzz off home before the German planes come back,' he said. Each boy threw his arms around Len's neck and gave him resounding double-cheek kisses, French style, Len was even more embarrassed than surprised; nobody had kissed him in many a year and he was touched by the natural gesture. He often thought of it during the next four years. It became something to cling to.

Next day, May 28, the CO visited the company and explained the serious position. The brigade was encircled by the Germans and in the same region, around Lille, the entire French First Army was cut off. The British 5th and 50th Infantry Divisions had fired every gun they had and for a time managed to contain the advance of the German panzer divisions, under Erwin Rommel. Now the British local commander, one Bernard Montgomery, had decided that the only way out was 'a lightning and fighting dash' through the German lines to the Dunkirk perimeter. The CO shook hands with each man individually and wished them good luck. At midnight the brigade formed up in a solid column of vehicles; on each open truck a machine gun had been mounted on a tripod at the rear. Then, without lights, the trucks roared through the villages, taking the Germans by surprise. Some thought their own units were on the move while those who opened fire received heavy fire in return. By daybreak on May 29 the Middlesex was again in Belgium, north of Ypres on the La Panne road, and slowed up by refugee crowds with carts and prams.

A German Storch aircraft attacked the column and Len tried vainly to bring it down with rifle fire but was flung out of the truck and into nettles when the driver took violent evasive action. As the men approached La Panne, on the coast, they were shocked to see in the fields beside the road hundreds of abandoned British artillery pieces and anti-aircraft guns, gun-limbers and trucks, either set on fire or so damaged as to be useless to the enemy. Len, who always had an eye for the useful, found a Bedford truck and happily cruised along at the rear of the convoy; he was sure that things were not as bad as they

seemed and that his truck would be needed. Then Lieutenant
Beef saw him, ordered him back into his own vehicle and set
fire to the Bedford. Len felt sad and aggrieved.

Another German aircraft attacked, a Dornier D17 this time.
Len was one of the few men in the regiment who knew exactly
what was attacking them and he volunteered the information
that this particular plane was known as the 'flying pencil'.
Dropping bombs and firing machine guns, the pilot killed four
men from another regiment in the column. As it flew over the
Middlesex, Corporal Stevens opened up with his Vickers which
was mounted on the roof of the truck cab and fired 500 rounds
– a full belt – at it. He cursed in frustration as he ran out of
ammunition but at that moment the tail of the plane started to
break away, then the whole tail section fell off and the Dorner
plunged into a field. A survivor climbed frantically from the
wreckage and with his hands in the air ran towards the
Middlesex men. As he approached, the Dornier burst into
flames and the Tommies heard the screams of the trapped crew.

'Kamerad!' the German cried in surrender.

'I'll give you kamerad, you bastard!' said Corporal Stevens
and with a .38 revolver he shot the man right between the eyes.
The fact that he had not long before taken the revolver from the
corpse of a British officer may have had something to do with
his forthright action.

'Come on!' Corporal Stevens shouted. 'Bring a couple of
shovels and bury him.'

The others did not exactly approve of Stevens' action; it was
not according to the rules of warfare. But on May 26, in the
village of Paradis, near Merville in northern France, the
Germans had lined up ninety prisoners of the 2nd Battalion the
Norfolk Regiment; then they mowed them down with machine
guns.*

* Two of the Norfolk men feigned death and were rescued by French people
who witnessed the massacre. They lived to bring evidence against the
principal SS officer responsible and after trial he was hanged.

Len's company drove along the coastal road towards Furnes, negotiating with difficulty the many roadblocks set up by their retreating comrades. At one crossroads Lieutenant Lyons stopped the convoy and went forward to reconnoitre. He stood there, legs wide, hands holding binoculars to his eyes and as the soldiers watched a single shot rang out – and Lyons crumpled. Lieutenant Parsy, promoted from his former rank as Regimental Sergeant Major, ran forward and bent over Lyons' still form. Another shot – and he fell across the body. Both officers had been killed by a sniper posted to watch the crossroads. Wriggling forward, soldiers dragged the bodies back and buried them, leaving their identity discs attached to makeshift crosses. The trucks roared across the crossroads without trouble; snipers rarely linger after two shots in such a position.

Passing through Furnes the Middlesex found many British dead on the pavements then took the road to Dunkirk, turning off after a while to follow a narrow track to a canal bank. Here the men were ordered to dig in. They were holding the Germans so that the bulk of the Army could escape; on that day alone 47,300 toops were evacuated from Dunkirk. Next day 56,000 would be taken off the beaches. Lieutenant Peters came along the line of dirty, sweating men. 'Can anybody here drive?' he called.

'Yes, I can!' Len was quick to answer. Driving before digging any day!

'Right,' the lieutenant said. 'Go back about twenty yards along the track, turn right and behind a house you'll find our first aid truck. Get in it and if anybody is injured you will drive them to the regimental aid post.'

Len did as ordered and when behind the steering wheel tried the engine. It started at once but as he turned it off two neat round holes appeared in the truck's woodwork close to his head. Almost simultaneously Len heard Sergeant Fuller shout, 'Get down off that truck, you idiot! Don't you know you're being fired at?'

Diving off the truck, Len dashed to where the sergeant stood behind cover. 'The last driver was shot dead in that truck five minutes ago,' he said. 'You don't know how lucky you are.' In fact, Len was beginning to realise that luck played a large part in war. That fact was to be driven home to him over and over.

A German creeping artillery barrage started and Len was one of a dozen soldiers who found refuge in a cellar, where they pessimistically discussed their chances of returning to Blighty. Their talk was cut short by a tremendous crash mixed with cordite fumes and dust and Len had the sensation of falling into a bottomless pit. He groped and clawed his way out of the wreckage to find that the front of the house had taken a direct hit. One man was unconscious and he was put on a stretcher. Sergeant Fuller ordered Len to drive him to the RAP, 'in the centre of town.'

Len had confidently volunteered as a driver but his experience was limited to one hour, the hour he had spent in the commandeered Bedford, without a single serious lesson. At that time army trucks had to be double declutched when changing down in gear, a process that required much practice. Len could not double declutch so once he had found top gear he left it there, using the choke to pick up speed on the corners and whenever he had to slow down. This kept him at about forty miles an hour. He rounded a corner to find a barricade across the road with just enough room at one side for a very slow moving vehicle to pass through. For Len that option had come too late; he hit the barrier at speed, and smashed carts and furniture hurtled across the street. Two French gendarmes, certain that this was the leading assault vehicle of the expected German blitzkrieg, took off. With debris stuck to the truck, Len found the aid post, where two British doctors were trying to cope with heavy casualties.

'I've got a wounded man in my truck,' he reported to one of them.

'Badly wounded?'

'We can't see any injuries, but he's unconscious.'

'See one of the orderlies and bring him in,' the MO ordered.

The busy orderly was equally curt. 'Right, grab one end of this stretcher and we'll carry him in,' he told Len.

Together they went to the truck and Len lowered the tail board and gestured into the back. The truck was empty.

'Well, where is he?' the orderly said impatiently.

'Blimey, he's hopped it,' Len said disbelievingly.

'Ar you some sort of nut?' the orderly snapped.

Len scratched his head under his helmet. 'He must have come to his senses during the journey and jumped out.'

'Look here!' the orderly snapped. 'We've got our hands full looking after the wounded. There's no time for playing jokes. Take your truck and get to hell out of here.'

Len kept looking into the back of the truck, wondering if the man had been thrown out when he rammed the barricade. There was nothing to do but return to the company's position; but the problem troubled him so much that he did not concentrate on his route back. An officer ran into the middle of the road and urgently waved him down. Len was astounded to see that the officer was a red-tabbed general and he threw a quick salute.

'Well, soldier,' the general said, 'where the devil do you think you're going?' But he did not sound angry and he swung in beside Len on the seat. Reflecting on the strangeness of war, which brought him into close contact with a general, Len explained that he was returning to his regiment.

'You won't reach your unit this way,' the general said. 'You're heading straight for the Germans. In fact, there's nothing beyond this point but the Germans and you should have turned right about half a mile back.' He dropped off the truck and said, 'Good luck.'

Len followed his directions, found his unit and parked the truck behind a building. During his absence the Germans had been dropping leaflets calling on the Allied soldiers to surrender. Each leaflet had a small map showing the Dunkirk perimeter with the message, 'Surrender to our troops and you will be treated as a brave enemy who fought and lost.'

While the Tommies were making ribald comments about what they would do with the propaganda leaflets, a low-flying Junkers 88 appeared with smoke pouring from its engine. A Hurricane was still firing its eight machine guns into the Junkers and the soldiers cheered themselves hoarse. This was the only time they were to catch sight of a modern Allied fighter during the whole of the campaign. Most of them were by now singing a ribald song, the chorus line of which was 'That fuckin' RAF is far away.'

With the Dunkirk evacuation under way, the Middlesex Regiment and other units held the perimeter and that summer's evening German guns pounded them hard, following with a creeping barrage which brought each salvo closer than the one before. Len threw himself into the soft earth of a ditch and dug furiously. As the shelling ceased he rose above the ditch to peer through the smoke – and a sniper's bullet whipped close to his head. Len dived and three minutes later tried for another view. The enemy marksman was watching and another bullet cracked past. This time Len remembered his training and crawled about ten yards along the ditch before he tried to snatch a glimpse of his enemy. For a third time a bullet just missed him.

'This is beyond a bleedin' joke!' Len said savagely. Keeping his head well below cover, he raised his rifle and fired all eleven rounds in the direction of the sniper. Then he lifted his steel helmet on the end of his rifle – and no shot came. Relieved, Len scrambled from the ditch and bolted for better shelter near a building and a truck.

It was soon one o'clock on the morning of May 30 and the protection of night lay over the British lines, though at this time of year night was short and often frighteningly transparent. Two men staggered out of the gloom and Len ran to help. Lieutenant Peters and Sergeant Fuller had been caught by a mortar bomb blast. The officer, wounded in the arm, said, 'Assist Sergeant Fuller first, Arlington, he's more critical than I am.'

The sergeant gave Len a twisted smile. 'The bastards have taken a lump out of my arse.' Len found that a chunk of bomb had mangled the fleshy part of Fuller's buttocks and he was losing blood so freely his trousers were soaked in it. Len got him into the truck where he lay on his stomach on some blankets. 'You're taking me to the RAP?' he asked.

'There is no RAP,' Len said. From experience he already knew that the only medical help was in the town.

Private Smith, who had been staring agape at the wounded men, said quickly, 'I know where to find the RAP, I can take them straight to it.'

Len knew this was a lie but he also knew that this was no time for an argument. If Smith wanted to run from the action than perhaps he could find help for the injured men. Lieut. Peters climbed into the cab and the truck moved off slowly, without lights.

The platoon was now under the command of Lance-Corporal Knowlan, who was understandably nervous in this emergency. 'Dawn's not far off,' he said to the worried Tommies. 'The Germans are sure to put in an attack at first light.' He ordered everybody to the machine gun positions near the canal and put the riflemen in position to support the gunners. 'First light is about an hour off,' he said and looked anxiously through the gloom. 'I wonder what's going on.' After a pause, 'There are some of our blokes along the canal . . . Guardsmen, I think.' In this command predicament the lance-corporal could think of no more welcome sight than Guardsmen, preferably an officer. The Middlesex men peered where he pointed and they too saw shadowy figures moving on the canal path.

'I'd feel a lot easier if I knew what they were doing,' Knowlan said. 'You, Len! You nip down there and see if you can find an officer and tell him what the position is up here.' Len had no doubt why he had been chosen; he was the youngest member of the platoon and the least likely to argue; older soldiers might well have disobeyed a mere lance-corporal. But he didn't mind; slinging his rifle over his shoulder and hooking his thumb under the strap he set off to stroll up the canal. He wore only his service belt with the bayonet in the scabbard, though he had twenty rounds of ammunition in the large front pocket of his battledress.

The shadowy forms in the distance were becoming more distinct – and obviously so had Len, for the men faded back into the shadows. A large barn next to the canal bank loomed into sight, with one of the big doors partly open. In its shadows stood two men, straining forward. Len was about to make a casual challenge, when one of the men said, 'Achtung! Englander!'

5

IN THE BAG

The harsh, abrupt German exclamation shocked Len into immobility. With his rifle still slung, he saw that he was only three feet from two Nazi officers, both of whom were pointing Lugers at him. 'Lummy, now I've blown it!' he told himself.

At a word of command from one of the officers a squad of soldiers came rushing from the barn to snatch away Len's rifle and give it to the officer. He ejected the rounds one by one and counted them as they fell on the towpath. When he had counted eleven, the maximum, he said, 'Gute!' He meant that he believed that Len had not been shooting at the Germans.

Beside the bank was a rubber dinghy and the officer motioned Len into it with his pistol; he and four of his men followed. Len was tense and expectant, knowing that thirty yards away two British heavy machine guns covered the canal. Half way across the canal he heard what he was expecting to hear – Corporal Knowlan's command, 'Fire!'

Tracer rounds flashed and cracked and one German pitched into the bottom of the boat while the others paddled frantically for the opposite bank. The boat, though hit many times, was unsinkable. For once, Len was glad that his mates were not shooting straighter. As the boat hit the bank the officer pointed up the slope with his pistol and snapped at Len, in English, 'Quick!'

Still under fire, Len was happy to oblige; and he beat the Germans in the race to the shelter of the bank, where he found a mass of infantry crouching as they waited to make an assault crossing. Len joined his officer captor while the other Germans eyed him curiously. Len was grinning cheerfully at them, on

the assumption that it was safer to be friendly, when the Luger
was jammed into his ear.

'Cigarettens?' the officer said.

Len thought he might have been more polite with his request but
he duly brought out a crumpled packet of Gold Flake. The officer
took one and the offered the packet around; nobody wanted
to smoke so he returned the packet to Len. This performance
was twice repeated within the next twenty minutes, after which
Len motioned to the officer to keep the packet. He reckoned that
before long the Luger might actually go off in his ear.

The Middlesex machine guns were still firing intermittently
and their chatter gave Len an idea, though it depended on his
being able to make the German officer more affable. He
pointed to the German eagle surmounted by a swastika above
the officer's breast pocket and said, 'Pilot?' When the German
seemed perplexed, Len added, 'Airman? Aeroplane?'

'Lieutenant, Germany Army,' the officer replied in a gruff but
reasonably friendly tone.

Len did a pantomime, gesturing across the canal to the
machine guns and gradually getting across the idea that he
could stop the firing – if he could be allowed to cross the canal.
Not that Len was serious; when he was back with his mates he
intended to show the gunners exactly where the Germans were
sheltering. But the lieutenant was interested in his idea. He
handed his pistol to a soldier with orders to keep Len covered
and crawled away to consult other officers.

When he returned it was only to mutter, 'Machine guns
kaput,' after which he resumed his place. And it was true – the
British guns were silent. The German troops moved off in single
file, crawling on all fours like huge dogs. Len thought many of
them were drunk or drugged. And then he heard a frightening
dog-growl behind him. Len twisted round to see a big Nazi
coming towards him with a fighting knife between his teeth
and a nasty look on his face beneath the camouflage blacking.
As Len flipped into position to face the man his hand came into
contact with his bayonet scabbard and he realised that he was
still armed. He jerked out the weapon and rose on one knee,

confident that given an even chance he could fight off his attacker. Then came a roar from the lieutenant and again Len found himself looking down the Luger barrel as the officer angrily held out his other hand for the bayonet.

'Half a mo!' Len said indignantly, 'What about that two-faced bleeder?' And he pointed to the enemy soldier.

The officer gave a curt order in German but the man ignored him, brushed him aside and took a swipe at Len with the knife. Len rolled sideways as the officer screamed another order and fired a shot into the air. The soldier dropped the knife and slowly raised his hands. The lieutenant, carefully covering him, uttered a few sentences quietly, then screamed at him again and finally struck him twice, open-handed, across the face. Len was sure that the German soldier had had an even narrower escape than he had; a Luger bullet might well have gone into his brain. The officer threw Len's bayonet into the canal.

Daylight had come and the officer beckoned Len to follow him, with two other German officers, across a field towards a farm building. A terrific screech tore the air and a heavy shell exploded only yards away. The Germans had flung themselves flat but Len remained standing, to the astonishment of the Germans who shook their heads in disbelief. On this occasion Len was not just being brave; he was still in a state of shock from being taken prisoner – the shock known only to other soldiers who have suffered the experience. He just could not believe what had happened to him a mere thirty minutes before. But his senses were sharp and when he saw the Germans' gesture of disbelief he had the incongruous thought that they were at least human.

The small party reached an outhouse which was none too safe as British bullets cracked through its open spaces. The lieutenant handed Len over to a guard, shook his hand grimly, said 'Good luck', and was gone. He was one of the very few civilised Germans Len was to encounter or even to hear about throughout the war.

His new guard was almost a Fritz caricature, a man in his fifties with a huge walrus moustache and beefy features. Len quickly assessed him as a music hall type of Hun who would give no real trouble. He was wrong. The guard jabbed his rifle muzzle into Len's ribs and shouted 'Raus! Raus!', making it clear that he wanted Len to run in front of him along a narrow track. Len, a real runner, soon knew from the angry shouts behind him that he was moving too fast, so at a jog prisoner and escort reached Furnes, whose streets were littered with bicycles, stolen by the advancing Germans to speed their advance and then abandoned when contact had been made with the British.

Fritz pointed to a bike leaning against a garden fence and motioned Len to mount. 'Well, if you insist,' Len said, 'but the bleeding thing has a puncture. Comprenez? Puncture?'

The German did not comprehend and shouted long and loud in German. Len sighed, shrugged and waited – which the guard took to be disobedience. He put his rifle to his shoulder, curled his finger around the trigger and took steady aim. 'All right, you great oaf,' Len said. 'Keep your shirt on.'

He started to pedal slowly along the road, the flat wheel going click-thump click-thump on the cobbles. Whenever Len glanced around he saw the rifle aimed straight at him. 'Dumb bloody German,' he muttered disgustedly.

After 500 yards or so the German noticed the flat tyre, yelled 'Halt!' and procured another bike for Len, as well as one for himself. As he mounted he warningly patted his rifle, resting across the handlebars, and again shouted 'Raus!'

An hour later he handed Len over to a German Intelligence HQ established in a small farm. A Nazi officer smiled at him and said in unaccented Englis, 'Welcome to the German Army. Come inside – some friends of mine wish to speak to you.'

'If they're friends of yours they aren't friends of mine,' Len said to himself as he followed the officer into a small room where two other officers sat at a table. Above and behind him, Len noted, was a portrait of Adolph Hitler, and he restrained himself from making the British Army's standard crude military gesture. The whole thing was unreal and he felt as if he had strayed into a film set.

The three officers, all young and handsome, nodded to him in a friendly way and the one in the middle, opening a folder, said, 'Now, just a few routine questions. First, what is your rank and number?'

'Arlington, private, number 6203442,' Len said.

The officer wrote down the details and asked casually, 'And your regiment?'

Len was a trained soldier; he knew very well that under the Geneva Convention a prisoner was required to give only his name, rank and number. In exaggerated Cockney he said, 'I'm sorry, but I don't fink dat I should answer dat.'

This produced an angry response from the only officer who had not yet spoken. Thumping the table with clenched fist, he shouted, 'Speak the King's English if you please!'

His colleagues thought that this was a great joke and they laughed uncontrollably for two or three minutes. Len also thought that the German's comment was funny but he decided not to provoke him by laughing. After a while the first officer said, 'You need not worry about giving away military secrets. We already have all the answers. Your unit is the Middlesex Regiment, stationed at Gosport before the war. Your first battalion is in Hong Kong. As you see, the questions are merely routine; you will not be telling us anything that we do not already know. But I would like to remind you that the treatment you will receive as a prisoner of war largely depends on this interview.'

Len nodded with exaggerated understanding. He listened to a lot of questions about the training methods of the British Army and wrily reflected that if he told the sorry truth about these methods these highly professional Germans would hardly believe him. He evaded their questions by asking some of his own. Once he said, 'You all speak very good English; *are* you English by any chance?'

This was good for another laugh and the spokesman said, 'No, we aren't English, but we did go to Cambridge.' They gave up the pointless questioning and summoned the guard. As he slauted, the three officers jumped up and in unison, gave the Nazi salute and shouted 'Heil Hitler!'

'Lord,' Len said to himself, 'If the boys could see me now with this bunch!'

At the back of the building the guard allowed Len to sit on a doorstep. It was forty-eight hours since he had slept and he was desperately tired. Fritz was also sleepy and prisoner and guard waged private battles to stay awake. Len went off first but awoke after a while to see that Fritz was snoring, and that his rifle had slipped from his fingers and was lying against his leg. Aircraft engines woke Len again and he saw in the distance four Bristol Blenheim bombers raiding enemy anti-aircraft guns. Apparently, the war was not entirely lost. One of the officers came into the yard, saw Fritz asleep and with a conspiratorial wink at Len he carefully lifted the rifle and took it inside, where he watched from a window. Fascinated, Len watched, too, and after a while the sleepy German stirred, awoke with a start and glanced quickly at Len and the guiltily at the HQ. Settling back comfortably, he groped for his rifle. Not finding it, he sat up with a violent start and jerked his head from left to right and back again as he looked for it. Impassively, Len saw the big man's face turn grey with fear as he eyed Len narrowly, suspecting that his prisoner had the rifle concealed behind him.

At that point the episode stopped being a joke. The officer appeared and shouted a series of commands. Fritz stood bolt upright, two other soldiers appeared at the double and he was marched away under arrest.

Len had little time to reflect about the incident. He too was marched away – this time to an army Volkswagen; he was ordered into the front seat while a German sat in the back with a Schmeisser sub-machine gun. Len was beginning to feel that he was the only British prisoner in France, especially when he saw the farmer's wife crying, and dabbing her eyes with a handkerchief. 'I'll be blowed,' he said, 'She's crying for me!' This was flattering but alarming.

As they sped along the main road they overtook a long military convoy and the officer said, 'You see the lies that the BBC is telling the British people. It says we have no petrol but we have all that we need. When we take the Channel ports it will be England's turn to feel our blockade.'

Reaching Dixmuide, in Belgian Flanders, the car stopped

outside a school building taken over by German field police. Two of them, distinguished by the crescent-shaped plaques they wore on steel chains around their necks, spoke with the officer and then approached Len, who was lounging near the car. They eyed him suspiciously and one of them thrust his hand into the large front pocket of Len's battledress trousers and brought out the handful of cartridges which Len had forgotten about and he whistled inwardly in alarm. Both Feldpolizei shouted and screamed and one smashed a clenched fist into Len's face, knocking him down. Wincing in pain, Len saw two revolvers aimed at him but the officer quickly intervened and placated the angry field police.

'Why didn't you give up those cartridges the moment you were taken prisoner?' he demanded.

'I just forgot,' Len said.

The officer shook his head impatiently, 'You are a very lucky man. Those policemen could have shot you out of hand and probably would have done so, had I not been present.'

Len could only nod his thanks. For the second time in twenty-four hours an enemy officer had saved his life. He was kept waiting for a few hours in a classroom and was then ordered into the back of an ambulance packed with seriously wounded Germans, several with limbs missing. Len was pleased to see that some British shooting had been accurate. The wounded men were cheerful and one gave Len a square of chocolate. 'For you the war is over, Tommy,' he said. Len had to admit that it seemed that way.

The driver started off and nobody spoke much during the hour's bumpy ride. The ambulance stopped and Len was ordered out. As he left, a wounded German whispered, 'Auf Wiedersehen, Tommy.'

'So long, mate,' Len said. 'Keep your pecker up.'

His guard marched him through the gates of a disused factory, stacked with packing cases labelled with the names of parts for British Fairy Battle bombers. Once inside, with the gates locked behind him, Len was free to wander about the place, which already had many occupants. In fact, the French 51st and 52nd regiments of infantry had surrendered themselves as complete units; they even had their field kitchens. An English-speaking captain took him to the cookhouse where he was given a mess tin of boiled macaroni with one sardine. Len, unfed for two days, wolfed it ravenously. The French officer, seated beside him, said, 'The war is as good as over, you know.'

Surprised, Len said, 'The war has only just begun.'

'France will fall within a few days,' the Frenchman said decisively. 'Then there will be nothing to stop the Germans crossing the Channel.' And he added, 'We have been sold out by our governments.'

'You might have been, mate,' Len said. 'But the British navy is still around.'

'And how will it stop thousands of parachutists being dropped from the skies?'

'Britain will never surrender to the Nazis,' Len assured him. 'It will fight to the bitter end.'

'Did you know that Prime Minister Chamberlain is out and that Winston Churchill has taken over?' the Frenchman asked. In fact, Neville Chamberlain had resigned as Prime Minister on May 10 and Churchill had formed a coalition government.

'I've been a bit busy lately to hear the news,' Len said wrily. 'But if Churchill is now Prime Minister we will certainly win the war. Churchill is a fighter. He will hammer the Nazis with a fist of steel. I tell you, he'll give the bastards what for.'

The captain laughed. 'You are a remarkable nation and you have more confidence in your government than we have in ours.'

A commotion at the factory gates ended their conversation. About twenty Germans were herding a dozen British soldiers into the compound; hands behind their heads, the Tommies were pushed into a tight circle and ordered to sit down, with four soldiers guarding them.

'Get rid of your helmet,' the captain advised Len, 'or they will put you with those prisoners. Make the most of your chances and keep out of sight among our men.' Len dumped his steel helmet on a pile of rubbish and hoped that his British battledress would pass unnoticed amid the French khaki.

On that warm night of June 1 Len slept on the cement floor,

using his tunic as a pillow. The guards shouted everybody awake at six a.m. and it was clear that there was to be a general clean out. In the confusion Len, feeling that he had been a prisoner long enough, scrambled under a large heap of British haversacks and gas respirators. Then he waited patiently for the factory to become silent. Hours later, he cautiously broke cover, his quick mind making plans to get out of the town, into the country and across the open fields to Dunkirk. As he walked quietly down the long factory a shout of 'Halte!' focussed his mind in quite a different direction.

An officer, much silver braid proclaiming his seniority, approached from a doorway and said in an amused tone, 'Ah, a British escaper, yes?'

'No sir,' Len said, as if offended by the idea. 'I woke up this morning to find the factory deserted and the guards gone.'

The officer laughed. 'Oh, I see. So now you wish to give yourself up. I think that can be arranged. We must find some transport so that you can rejoin your comrades.' He tapped the young soldier on the shoulder. 'It would be stupid of you to try to escape in full daylight and in your British uniform from the centre of an occupied town, don't you agree?'

Len saw the logic of the argument and accompanied the officer through the factory, out of the gates and into a side turning where a soldier sat in the saddle of a motor cycle combination. The officer motioned Len into the passenger seat. 'Good luck,' he said. 'Let's hope that this war will soon be over.'

Len nodded affably enough but he said to himself, 'And let's hope you stop a bullet right between the eyes.'

Three miles out of town the motor cyclist caught up with the long column of trudging prisoners and indicated that Len should join it. He found himself with the French soldiers of the 51st and 52nd regiments as well as many Belgian troops. The dusty, thirsty and dispirited men were well guarded with German guards on bicycles on either side of the column and about ten yards apart. The day was bright and hot and as the defeated men wound their way through village after village the people came out to look at them in bewildered and sympathetic silence.

About noon the Germans called a halt of fifteen minutes and many men collapsed by the roadside; others, including Len, pushed and shoved to get a drink from a cattle trough. Then came the order 'Raus! Raus! Los! Schnell!' and the march of defeat went on.

By evening the Frenchmen, mostly middle-aged, were panting in distress and some were barely able to hobble.

Len Arlington reflected that he had not taken his boots off for three weeks – a fact that said little for the junior leaders who should have seen that their men changed their socks and washed their feet at least once a day. But Len was in good condition and his feet gave him no trouble; at twenty he was in no real difficulty that steaming day, while older men around him were in dire distress from pain and discomfort.

At ten p.m. that evening the men were marched into a field and grouped into their various nationalities, while guards patrolled the perimeter. The Germans had commandeered all the bread from village bakeries and now came the share-out. The Belgians were served first, one loaf among ten men; then about half the French were served before the supply ran out. This left many French and all the British hungry. Len was very hungry as he had eaten practically nothing for a week.

A tall prisoner with a large beard joined Len that night. A Russian by birth, he had volunteered to serve in the French army and now, convinced that the war was over, he proposed to escape that night. He gave Len a small groundsheet and shook his hand and Len saw no more of him. Sporadic machine gun fire, as the guards fired at shadows, gave the prisoners an uneasy sleep and at dawn they were on the road again.

Early in the afternoon a French Senegalese soldier, panting and unable to take another step on his blistered and bloody feet, fell out by the roadside. Two guards rushed up and threatened to shoot him if he did not rejoin the column. A group of Tommies, grabbing sticks and stones, formed a defensive circle around the black man. The situation was ugly as both sides threatened each other – then the Germans backed away. For two hours the British soldiers took turns to carry the helpless Senegalese, their spirit roused by the continual jeering of the Germans; then the Germans allowed them to put him in a truck together with other elderly exhausted prisoners.

By four that afternoon the column was disintegrating into straggling groups as the French prisoners staggered in blind exhaustion. At this point some NCO among the British took formal control. He formed the men into fours, as if they were marching in a parade, and somehow induced them to sing Tipperary and other marching songs. Even the French rallied under this injection of morale and many called 'Bravo, les Anglais!'

That evening the British were separated from the French and Belgian soldiers and marched to a house in Oudenarde where German newsmen were waiting to question and photograph some of the first prisoners taken at Dunkirk. One eyed Len and said, 'How old are you?'

'Twenty-five,' Len said.

'Are you a conscript?'

'No, I'm a volunteer,' Len said proudly.

The German sneered at him and moved on to other prisoners, while another Tommy said to Len, 'Blimey, you don't look twenty-five.'

'I'm twenty really,' Len said, 'but that's none of their bleedin' business.' It was characteristic of the man; weaponless and a captive, he was fighting back in the only way open to him. He tried it again that evening, in a different way. The men were marched to another house where two Belgian civilians brought in a jug of what seemed like milk but turned out to be sour butter milk, which the British could not manage to drink. A feldwebel (sergeant) ordered Len and another prisoner up the stairs to a room which a Belgian medical orderly was preparing for the arrival of German wounded. The sergeant shoved a broom into Len's hands and shouted at him. Len did not comprehend a word but found the bullying performance comical, so he shouted back in what he thought sounded like gutteral German, 'Blaas! Blaas! Blaas!'

The feldwebel was furiously angry. Grasping his rifle by the barrel he bashed Len repeatedly on the shoulders, shouting at him all the time. After a while he calmed down a little and stomped off down the stairs while the terrified Belgian helped Len to his feet and patted him on the back.

'That bloody Nazi has no sense of humour,' Len said, wincing with pain.

'*Comment?*' the Belgian replied.

'As common as they come,' Len agreed.

When Len and the other British were returned to the POW compound they found that the evening meal – a raw herring for each man – had already been distributed to the Belgians and French. Once more the British went hungry. On the second day a thin watery soup was served out, once more to the Belgians first and then to the French. Yet again the supply ran out before the Tommies could be served.

A large canal ran through the grounds of the compound, which was really factory grounds, and the Germans allowed their prisoners to splash around in it as much as they wanted, probably because it kept them out of mischief. About fifty yards away a road bridge spanned the canal and here the local girls gathered to watch hundreds of men swimming, diving and generally fooling about in the water – all of them completely naked. From their laughs and shouts of 'Ooh, la, la!' it was apparently an amazing sight and some of the soldiers did their best to make it even more startling for the girls.

Among the prisoners, Len found another Middlesex man, Pte. Knight, and they teamed up to go on a 'food patrol' to some houses further down the canal. As swimming was the only way to reach the houses, they left their uniforms with another soldier on the promise of a share of their finds. This time they kept their underpants on and swimming casually they stretched the distance btween themselves and the guards. When they had reached danger point they swam submerged, coming up close to the bank for a gulp of air. In this way they reached the backyard of a house overlooking the canal. The building was empty but in a hutch they found a rabbit and a young cockerel and both were quickly killed. Then the two men swam back, Len with the rabbit, Knight with the cockerel. They were cooked in mess tins and shared out as far as they would go; Len's portion was a rabbit leg. It was the only real food he had in the ten days he spent as a prisoner.

At six a.m. on the third morning the prisoners were forced on the march again and this time the British began the day with a song – the *Beer Barrel Polka*. The officer in charge of the column joined in and even shouted orders to the guards to sing. After a while the Tommies started on Arthur Askey's *Run Adolph, run Adolph, run, run, run*. The song was well known to the Germans as *Run rabbit, run rabbit, run, run, run* so they kept the British company in the tune, not realising that the Tommies were ridiculing the Fuhrer.

By noon that day the column was approaching Renaix and to show the townspeople that they were not downhearted the British broke into the most popular song of the first nine months of the war – '*We're going to hang out our washing on the Siegfried line ... if the Siegfried line's still there ...*'

The German guards were so much in the mood that they sang this song too – until the officer realised what was happening. He screamed apoplectically for the singing to stop. Guards ran up and down the column, thumping their rifle butts into men's backs and threatening them with the bayonet. But the French and Belgians joined in the tune and the Germans could not stop the noise. The people of Renaix leaned from their windows or ran into the street with shouts of 'Voilà, les Anglais!' and 'Bravo, Anglais!'

They quickly subsided as they saw the Germans knocking prisoners down with their rifles and women began to cry. The soldiers continued to sing from time to time but no longer did the Germans join in. The officer in charge increased the pace of march and ordered the guards to fire their rifles over the heads of the prisoners to make sure there was no further commotion and emotion as they passed through Ellezelle, Lessines and Enghien. As darkness was falling at the end of another long, hot day the men were directed to a field near Enghien. Two guards stood at the entrance, hitting the prisoners with their rifle butts as they passed through. Len noticed that a Senegalese held his steel helmet by the chin strap and as the guard bashed him with the rifle butt the black man swung around and smashed him full in the face with the helmet. As he disappeared into the flock of prisoners the guard collapsed unconscious.

The Germans knew that any attempt to find the attacker was useless but next morning the ordinary guards were replaced by sinister looking SS troops, who were hell-bent on intimidation. They glowered and spat insults and fired machine gun bursts over the column. During the next day's march Belgian civilians placed buckets of water on the pavements so that the hot and exhausted soldiers could snatch a drink; they had to be very quick before the SS guards rode up and kicked the buckets over.

At noon a five-minute rest was permitted. Len, his chest heaving, lay on his back with the others, gazing up with relief at the blue sky, until there came the dreaded 'Raus! Raus!' Len pushed himself to his feet, swayed dizzily from the combined effects of heat, hunger and exhaustion, and pitched into a heap. Pain brought him back to consciousness – pain caused by an SS guard who was kicking him savagely in the ribs and shouting at him to get up.

'This is no bloody good, no bloody good at all,' he said grimly to himself as he staggered along. 'Young Len will have to do something about it.' And when, at a later stop, he again stood up too quickly and passed out he knew that he must act before he became too weak to move fast. Better to be shot attempting to escape than die of exhaustion and starvation.

While he was pondering, the column passed through Tubise and then Braine-L'Alleud – and there stood a signpost reading WATERLOO STATION 2K. The British managed a weak cheer at this. The following day a French officer collapsed and died by the roadside, an event which fired Len's escape resolve. The next day the guards were on foot, spaced out every thirty yards on either side of the column. As it reached a wooded area Len became alert and when he realised that the road was winding sharply he knew that this was the moment. On an S-bend the guard in front of Len turned around and walked backwards for

a pace or two as he glanced back along the column. As he
resumed his forward march Len gambled that the next guard
was out of sight in the bend. He took three or four quick
strides and made a flying leap into the foliage. Landing on all
fours in a dry ditch, he burrowed down among the summer
foliage and with thumping heart he waited tensely for the
column to pass. Such an escape attempt could inspire other
British to follow but Len remained alone. He knew that the
French and Belgians would not run because the Germans had
told them that they would be released in a matter of days. Len
was taking a big risk, for he well knew that squads of SS had
been detailed to follow the column and pick up escapers and
stragglers. Carefully, he moved deeper into the forest, found a
thick clump of bushes – and fell asleep. When he awoke a few
hours later he knew that he was really free.*

* In September 1939 26 Diehard officers and 742 other ranks had gone to
France. On June 11 1940, back in England the tally was 21 and 530: 4
officers and 12 men had been killed; the remainder, including many
wounded, were taken prisoner.

6

ON THE RUN

For the first time in days Len was aware of the beauty of summer; until now it had just been a time of misery in the heat and dust and long days of trudging. As a prisoner he had not been aware of birds but now he heard them singing. Best of all, he was alone. Escaping alone took a rare kind of courage but Len was not aware of that; he knew only that by himself he had a better chance of getting away. Most men would have wanted the confidence which comes from company, not giving a thought to the problems this would impose on them. Len liked company but he did not need it.

Hearing the crackling of twigs and the mutter of voices he climbed high into a tree with the agility of a boy scrumping apples. Four British soldiers, other escapers on the run, came into sight. Len had not the slightest temptation to join them and as they passed beneath him he shook his head in sympathy. 'Poor mugs,' he said softly, 'the bloody Germans'll hear you coming a mile off.'

Exploring, Len found two cottages in a forest clearing; even better, they had vegetable gardens which stretched back to the forest. Flat on his stomach, he inched into the gardens and dug up some new potatoes which had been planted as seed, as well as some small carrots and onions. He found some water in a barrel at the end of the garden and drooling in anticipation, he crawled back into the forest, lit a fire and boiled the vegetables in his mess tin. The meal was unappetising but it reduced his hunger a little.

Heading in the reverse direction to that taken by the prisoners' column, Len emerged from the forest into a large open field shimmering with heat. The only cover between him and another patch of forest was a large chestnut tree and he headed for it, forcing himself to walk casually so as not to attract attention. When he was still twenty yards from the tree a truck roared out of the trees ahead and raced in his direction. He sprinted to the tree, hugged the trunk and peered around it. The truck was a British Bedford 15 cwt – but it was driven by a German soldier in field grey and beside him stood another soldier behind a machine gun mounted on a pivot. This man was sweeping the fields through field glasses. The driver approached to within yards of the big tree and drove a half circle around it as Len slid around the trunk. After a pause and some conversation the Germans drove back to the woods and when the sound of the engine faded away Len followed.

His vision distorted by the rising waves of heat and by his weariness, Len pressed on through the forest and approached a shed in another field. He was again lucky – the shed was full of dairy cattle. He selected a cow with full udders, urged her to her feet and with a skill that came from his earlier farming experience he filled his mess tin with her milk. He drank this on the spot and helped himself to a refill, though he repeatedly had to cuff away another friendly animal chewing at the back of his neck. Not until he was about to leave did Len discover that he had been irritating a fully-grown bull.

Back in the woods he lit a fire and boiled the rest of the milk, drank it as it cooled, stretched happily and felt ready to face further adventures. After a few miles' walk he came across a large chateau and scaled the iron railings surrounding it. Forcing a window, he found himself in a linen room and after further search located an enormous kitchen, complete with food lifts to carry meals to the dining room above. Not that Len was able to dine – in that vast place he could find nothing more than a single tin of small peas, which he swallowed at a gulp. Upstairs he found bedrooms vacated in haste, the bedclothes in disarray.

Len had never been in such a grand and opulent home and he treated himself to a private tour. The chapel was particularly intriguing; it had seating for at least fifty, with two rows of

seats for the choir, and an electric organ. In the upstairs hall he
came across a grand piano and seating himself with the air of a
concert pianist he tapped out, crudely but coherently, the notes
of Lieberstraum, learned years before at the Home. He laughed
aloud as the notes echoed ghostlike through the tall, silent
chambers. 'Len lad,' he said, 'you could have a lovely war if you
could go on living here. Wonder how much rent they're asking.'

Suddenly a dog barked outside. Len shut the piano and ran
for the stairs. He cleared them going down three at a time only
to be checked half way by a fox terrier which snapped and
barked at him. Standing statue-still, Len said softly, 'Nice
doggie, that's the boy! Uncle Len won't hurt you. Nice doggie.'
The dog went on barking and the sounds were alarmingly loud
in the silent house. 'You bleedin' little perisher!' Len hissed. 'I'll
break your flamin' neck!'

He was reaching cautiously for the animal when somebody
whistled shrilly. The dog gave a last bark, eyed Len malevolently
and reluctantly left him. Within a minute Len was down the
stairs and through the passages, not stopping until he had
scaled the railings safely and was in the woods.

In a small clump of trees he found in a ditch the fly-infested
corpses of two Germans, one still clutching his rifle. Len took it
and as it was in good working order he was tempted to keep it
but reluctantly put it down; he knew that if he were caught
with it he would be shot on the spot.

Nearby lay a Belgian greatcoat, with a major's crowns on
the epaulettes so Len promoted himself; the heavy coat would
be useful at night. He raided some more gardens with little
success and as dusk fell he approached an isolated farm, in
the hope that he would be taken for a Belgian escaper. A woman
of about forty answered his knock and Len held out his mess tin,
'De l'eau, s'il vous plaît, madame.' His French was adequate for
simple conversation.

Without a word she took the tin and Len heard her filling it at a
kitchen pump. When she returned and handed it to him she spoke
in Flemish and Len replied with a shrug. The woman changed to
French. 'Vous n'êtes pas Belge.' Her tone was suspicious.

Len took a chance. 'No, madame,' he said 'Je suis Anglais.'
And he opened the greatcoat to show his British uniform. The
woman became excited and her eyes glowed with welcome.
Throwing open the door she said urgently, 'Entrez, vite!' She
guided him to the kitchen where Len saw on the table a freshly
baked loaf of bread and some jam. The woman noticed his
almost hypnotised expression and said, 'My God, you must be
starving.' Motioning him to a chair she pushed him the loaf and
jam and Len, almost in a state of ecstasy, wolfed half of it.

The farmer came in from the fields and was not too alarmed
to find a British soldier in his kitchen, though he was surprised
that this soldier had survived for a full day on the run. German
patrols were everywhere, he said, and they were shooting
British soldiers on sight. 'Rest in our hayloft,' he suggested. 'Try
to get some sleep and I'll call you at midnight. It will be safer
to move then.'

Len was too weary to argue; anyway, he trusted these people.
The farmer took him to the hayloft and then removed the
ladder so that unwelcome visitors would not be tempted to
investigate the loft. Len dug a nest in the sweet-smelling hay,
pulled the overcoat over himself and was asleep in seconds.

Voices raided in angry argument awoke him and he saw that
it was broad daylight. Alarmed, he realised that he was hearing
shouts in German and peering through a crack he saw about
thirty gesticulating Germans surrounding the farmer's wife.
Followed by the woman's shrilly scolding voice, they spread out
to search the farm buildings. Len had no way out and as he
waited he said to himself, 'If you get out of this, Len, you won't
box yourself in again.'

A shouted command came from the farm entrance and an
officer appeared. The searching men came running to assemble
directly below the loft door behind which Len was crouching.
At another command they turned smartly into column and
marched out of the farm singing. Soon the farmer's wife came
with the ladder, bringing Len a bundle of clothing. 'It will be
dangerous for you in uniform,' she said. 'Come inside when
you have changed.'

The farmer's old clothing was a good fit except for the shoes, which were too tight but Len felt much more comfortable without his uniform and minus his identity disc. In fact, without a uniform his situation was really more dangerous; if captured in civilian clothing he could well be regarded as a spy and shot. Inside the house, when he had changed, another loaf of bread, jam and coffee awaited him.

'What did those Germans want?' he asked.

'Don't you worry about those animals,' the woman said contemptuously. 'They were after butter and fresh eggs and I told them there was nothing on this farm for the likes of them.' Len was impressed with her courage; she could have been shot for harbouring an escaper and the soldiers might well have beaten her up but she insulted them and ordered them off her property.

He went on westwards, in the general direction of home. Finding even the minor roads full of German troops and their transport he kept to the narrow country lanes. Detouring the town of Wavre, he entered a large forest where he found two woodcutters at work and they shouted a cheerful 'Bonjour!'

The moment Len replied, one of the woodcutters said, 'You're a soldier, aren't you, escaping from the Germans?'

Len admitted it and the three men sat and talked about the war. The woodcutters were worried when Len said that he proposed to reach Dunkirk. 'Don't try it,' the older one urged. 'You wouldn't have a chance. Hide in the woods until autumn and you will be safe until the British make a counter-offensive.'

And the other advised, 'Come and see the mayor. He's a good man and will help you.'

Len let them guide him to the mayor's house. He was absent but his wife was sympathetic and fulfilled Len's greatest need – for a pair of better-fitting shoes. While he tried on pair after pair the mayor's twin daughters, beautiful girls of eighteen, stood and gazed at the warrior escaper with tremendous admiration. They gave him a meal and then accompanied him to the edge of the town, from where they waved him off across the fields.

He covered a lot of ground that afternoon and towards evening, again in forest, he came to a small clearing where stood one of the most beautiful cottages he had ever seen. Built of stone, it sat in the centre of a rich and colourful garden, with wild roses climbing the walls. An elderly man stood at the garden gate and Len studied him for some time from the cover of the woods before he approached. Serious faced and worried, the man spoke to Len in Flemish and though he could not understand a word Len sensed trouble and tragedy. This became more evident when a girl aged about twenty-two appeared at the door, her blue eyes red and swollen with weeping. Len explained in a mixture of English and French that he was English and on the run from the Germans, 'les Allemands'. At this word the girl trembled uncontrollably and wrung her hands and her features were contorted in terror. The man cried, too, as he explained that a few days before a party of German soldiers had stormed into the house, raped the girl and shot dead her mother and brother when they tried to protect her. Every few minutes the girl uttered a heart-rending wail and Len thought that she was out of her mind. When her father spoke sharply to her she rallied and invited Len into the house and gave him a meal. He slept in a bed that night but his sleep was disturbed by the girl's nightmare screams.

The pair gave him bread and coffee in the morning. Feeling helpless and inadequate Len said, 'Courage,' in the French accent, and went on his own dangerous way. It hurt him to look back and wave goodbye for he felt the pair needed protection. He swore savagely about Nazi soldiers.

He detoured around Le Hulpe, entered the forest of Soignies and during the afternoon came to a bungalow, whose owner had left a note on the front door saying that he could be found at an address in Brussels. This was welcome news to Len for it meant that he would be undisturbed. He broke in by cutting out the metal gauze sheet which covered the pantry window with his penknife – which could have landed him in more serious trouble had his captors known about it. To his delight he found tins of sardines, packets of tea, a large tin of biscuits, coffee and plenty of red wine. After preparing a feast, he sat comfortably in a lounge chair, rested his feet on a hassock and toasted his absent host, 'Len Arlington of the Middlesex Regiment thanks you,' he said aloud, 'even if you do only drink lousy plonk.' After his meal of sardines, biscuits and wine he found a haversack and packed the entire stock of tinned food, biscuits and tea. Satisfied that he had caused no damage, he let himself out through the back door and finally he carefully replaced the wire gauze.

He reached the main Brussels–Charleville road, along which thundered an apparently never-ending convoy of German military transport. Slipping across the road between two trucks, Len walked still further west and reached Braine-L'Alleud. He recognised it at once – he had passed through it as a prisoner in the marching column. He wanted to put the place quickly behind him but was still on the pavement of the main street when a troop convoy overtook him. As German soldiers stared down at him he felt vulnerable and conspicuous, almost as if he were wearing a placard proclaiming BRITISH SOLDIER.

About fifty trucks had passed when the convoy slowed and came to a halt. Instantly hundreds of soldiers jumped down to stretch their legs, blocking the pavement and pushing civilians out of their way. Len, not wishing to be forced into confrontation by some Nazi bully, sat down on a doorstep next to a Belgian woman who was watching the Germans with passive contempt. He hoped that the Germans would take him to be just one more Belgian youth watching the soldiers. The woman tapped Len's haversack and asked if it held anything to eat. Alarmed, Len replied briefly and rudely and the woman said nothing more. After a while the troops climbed back into their trucks and the convoy moved off. When the last truck had gone Len stood up and said, 'Merci, madame.'

'You are not a Belgian,' she said.

'No,' Len admitted. 'I am an escaped British prisoner of war.'

The woman gave a startled bleat and shot into her house, slamming the door behind her. Len chuckled and pressed on, passing through Brain-Le-Chateau on the road to Tubise. A German motorcyclist passed him at high speed, then turned and drove back and Len saw from the neck chain and plaque that he was a military policeman. Pulling into the kerb, the MP lifted his goggles, pointed down the road and said, 'Tubise, m'sieur?'

'Oui! Oui!' Len almost shouted in his tension. 'Straight on!' And the MP roared off.

From Tubise, Len headed for Enghien on the Enghien–Halle road. Shouts of 'Raus! Raus! Schnell!' reached him and round a bend, approaching him, came another column of weary British and French prisoners under guard, yet another haul from the Dunkirk's debacle. Len's first impulse was to turn and run but he fought down his fear and went into his act as interested bystander. This was made simpler for him by a farmer who had pulled his horse and cart to the side of the road. Len leaned against the cart, pretending to be the farmer's boy.

He had a great urge to say something cheerful to the British prisoners – perhaps 'Chin up, mate,' or 'Don't let the bastards get you down.' Controlling the impulse, he watched until the end of the trudging column had disappeared.

After a night in a barn, with rats for company, Len used the open road and the safer fields and passed through one town after another – Enghien, Lessine, Ellezelle, Ronse, Niuekerke. That night a farmer and his wife, though terrified of discovery by the Germans, allowed Len to sleep in a barn. He awoke at dawn with a fearful headache, a sore throat, high fever and biliousness. When the farmer brought him a bowl of hot milk Len asked him if he could stay for the day but the worried man said that his wife had not slept at all and was a nervous wreck through anxiety; they dared not take the high risk of hiding him during the day. Too weak to argue, Len set off in drizzling rain and was soon soaked. After only a mile he collapsed in a heap and with a great effort of will he crawled into a field of corn only a foot high, where he lay shivering and sweating. A warm sun came out about noon and Len slept for four hours, waking up feeling rather better but very weak. Again he pushed on, using the road for easier travel. His route lay through Zuzeke, Berchem and Roulers; his ultimate destination was Dunkirk, now an obsession with him. He was convinced that the British were still fighting the Germans there because he could hear heavy gunfire from that direction.

On the outskirts of Berchem he took the Courtrai (Kortrijk) road and was within yards of the bridge over the Scheldt River when a stout fair-haired woman in her fifties stopped him. Looking sharply into his eyes, she said slowly and clearly, 'The German police are stopping everybody on the bridge to check their identity papers.'

Len squeezed her hand in thanks. 'I'm an escaped prisoner of war,' he said.

'I knew it,' she said tensely. 'That's why I warned you.'

Since Berchem was so dangerous Len turned back along the Ronse road and arrived at the small village of Ruien, where yet another civilian, a man of forty, stopped him. 'You are English, aren't you? Come home with me.'

This was Mr Brouke, who ran a farm with his sister. Len could stay there for a few days, they said, if he would help with the work; it was pointless for him to go to Dunkirk, as the British had evacuated it and fighting had ceased.

Len had lost track of the date, but it was already more than a week into June. The last evacuation ships had left Dunkirk on the night of June 3–4 and in all 338,226 British and 120,000 French and Belgian troops had been taken off. A total of 861 ships and many private craft had been employed and 243 had been sunk. The Germans captured Dunkirk on June 4, taking 40,000 French prisoners and great quantities of abandoned British equipment, including 2,472 guns and 84,427 vehicles and motorcycles. Large parts of the French army were still fighting further south, as well as another 30,000 British troops. The British prisoners Len had seen on the Enghien–Halle road were the last from Dunkirk and the first from the Somme fighting of June 5–8. Brouke knew enough of the true picture to convince Len that continuing on towards Dunkirk was pointless. Loss of his goal was a great shock and disappointment so he agreed to stay on the farm and was given a bunk in the stables.

The Broukes worked him hard, getting him up at four in the morning and keeping him on the job until eleven at night. Still, Len knew the work, he was fit, and most important he was safe.

Then the Broukes' attitude changed. They had been listening to German-controlled Belgian radio and a lot of clever propaganda was having its effect. While working in the cornfields with Len, Brouke said, 'France has capitulated. Germany has won the war.'

He had heard Marshal Petain's broadcast of June 20, in which he described the defeat of France as 'inevitable'; he had compared the 185 British, American and Italian divisions supporting the French army in May 1918 with the 10 British divisions of May 1940. When Brouke spoke to Len on June 22, France and Germany were signing an armistice agreement at Compiègne and the last of the French forces – 400,000 men in six armies – were surrendering in the Vosges pocket. Brouke was obviously convinced that the Germans had not simply conquered France but had won the war itself.

Len did not like this talk and he hated Brouke's defeatist attitude. 'But England still fights on,' he said.

'What can England do on her own against all the might of Germany?' the farmer said. 'The Germans will be in London within a month.' He laughed at the prospect.

Len was inexperienced in argument but he knew something of British history, 'England loses every battle except the last,' he said fiercely.

'Oh yes!' said Brouke, with a sneer. 'But England is not now conquering other countries. She is fighting for her life and nothing can stop the Nazis now.'

Len threw the farm fork at Brouke's feet. 'All right, you stay with your Nazi friends!' he said. 'I'll be on my way.'

Back at the farm, as he quickly gathered his few possessions, Len met Brouke's sister. 'You are leaving us?' she said.

'It is becoming rather unhealthy around here,' Len said. 'Yes, I must leave. Adieu.' And suddenly he realised where he must go – back to Gondecourt where the regiment had been based. He knew friendly people there and they would hide him. Gondecourt was in France on the other side of the border, and borders were dangerous, but Len didn't hesitate. He took the road to Orroir and found a small group of shops; his reserve rations had all gone and he was hungry so he entered a small grocery shop. The tinkling doorbell brought a woman of about seventy who asked, in French, 'Can I help you, M'sieur?'

'I would like some biscuits,' Len said.

The elderly woman smiled. 'Ah, you are English.' She reached out and squeezed his arm in welcome.

Len sighed, despairing of ever being a successful escaper if he was always so quickly identified. 'How did you know, madame?'

'I was in service in England for twenty years,' she said, 'and I came to know the British very well, and to admire them. Myself, I am Belgian but everybody around here calls me Aunt Marie. Come into the kitchen, it's safer there, and we can talk over a cup of tea.'

She had a comfortable home behind the shop and as they sipped their English tea, Len said that he proposed to cross into France.

'What, cross the frontier on foot!' Aunt Marie said. 'The Germans will suspect a man on foot.' She thought for a while and then said briskly, 'Well, rest a while and I'll get you something to eat.' Len was glad to rest and when he had eaten Aunt Marie's very full meal he was ready to go. He liked this gentle old lady and did not want to risk her safety.

But she kept him there by giving him one cup of tea after another. There was no hurry, she said, he had all the time in the world. He was still there in the evening when she casually announced that she had made up the bed in the spare room; he would be safe and she would call him in the morning. After the hard labour and lack of sleep on the Brouke farm Len dropped into instant sleep. Aunt Marie did not call him in the morning and the day was well worn when he awoke. He found her in the kitchen, where she served him breakfast and said decisively, 'You won't be able to go today, of course. You will have to stay to dinner because I have some friends coming to see if there is any way they can help you.'

She was busy during the day and Len sensed that he was the centre of her activity. Just before dinner Aunt Marie called him into the enclosed back garden, where an almost new bicycle was leaning against the wall. 'There you are!' she said triumphantly. 'With that you won't have any trouble getting into France – you'll be just like any Frenchman or Belgian.'

Len stared at the bike in disbelief; he had never owned a bicycle as good as this one and he could not understand why this old woman would want to give it to him. 'I don't know how to thank you,' he said.

'You just did so – and very well,' Aunt Marie said. 'There's just one problem – you can't leave until Monday morning. That's when two friends of mine will be able to take you across the frontier.'

'Just like that?' Len said. 'I hope they know the best way.'

'They should,' Aunt Marie said with a bright smile, 'They are professional smugglers.'

Once again Len tried to thank her in his clumsy soldier's way but Aunt Marie cut him short. 'Oh, do be quiet son. It's the least one can do.'

The weekend was peaceful, almost like a holiday, and war seemed very distant. By Monday Len was rested when the two smugglers arrived and were introduced. Now no time was wasted. Len wheeled out his bike. Aunt Marie kissed him and tried and failed to keep back her tears.

Len hugged her tightly. 'I love you, Aunt Marie,' he said. 'You're my sweetheart.'

'I love you too, son,' she said. 'Goodbye and God be with you.' Then, quickly, she went inside.

Len and his new friends reached the customs post just south of Dottignies and approached the two French officials who were watched from a short distance by two German soldiers, with rifles slung over their shoulders. 'Just do as we do,' one of the smugglers whispered, and gave the officials a breezy 'Bonjour'.

The customs men made a show of examining the men's papers and stood between the Germans and Len, who had no papers. 'You can ignore those two sausages,' the senior man said contemptuously, jerking his thumb at the Germans. 'They're just there for show.' And moments later Len, to his great delight and relief, was in France. He was sure that now all would be well.

The smugglers escorted him to Wattrelos and put him on the

right road for Leers, from where he reached the large town of Ascq, which was crowded with Germans who had been billeted there. Soon Len was in Lesquin and on the airfield he saw many Junker 87s and Heinkel 111s. Enemy activity was so brisk he was glad to put Lesquin behind him. But the next town, Seclin, was no comfort; the Germans had bombed to rubble the centre of the place, which Len had known so well. The memorial to the British troops who had liberated Seclin from German occupation in World War 1 had been pushed over. After this destruction and enemy vandalism Len wondered what he would find in Gondecourt, which the Middlesex men had regarded as their own town. With fast-beating heart he cycled up to the Cafe Ringot. All was so silent that he feared the worst, even as he nostalgically remembered how he and his mates had sung their hearts out in the place. Many of those comrades were dead or in captivity.

He passed through the low archway into the backyard where one of Grandmere Estelle's granddaughters, a girl of ten, was playing. She looked at Len blankly for a few moments then ran into the house shouting, 'Granny, the English are back! Here's Lee-on-ar!'

Len gave a great sigh of relief. He had not brought the army with him but he was among old friends. He had already had more narrow escapes than he could count, and he had learnt a lot. Let the Nazis come. He was sure that he could evade them but as the family rushed out to greet him he was aware of a terrible responsibility. Whatever happened, he must not put his friends at risk.

7

'O.K. TOMMY!'

Within minutes of Len's arrival the Ringot family had assembled
– Grandmère Estelle, Florentin and his wife Zelfa, and their sons
Edouard and Jean-Marie, and Desiré, Estelle's forty-five-year-old
son, who had been discharged from the army. Len had only seen
him in his uniform, now he was wearing blue overalls. Desiré
opened the cafe, which had been closed since the Middlesex
Regiment had departed, and everyone drank Len's health.

The jollity was brief for everybody knew how serious the
situation was, and the French were in a state of shock. They had
been living a delusion – that France was impregnable. The
arrogance, obstinacy and short-sightedness of the French generals
had been astonishing. Only days before the German Panzer Corps
poured through the Ardennes Forest, General Huntziger,
commander of the French 2nd Army, had ordered the removal of
all anti-tank obstacles from the roads in his area on the grounds
that their existence was contrary to standing orders. Marshall Petain
had contemptuously dismissed the value of armoured vehicles and
aircraft in a major European war. And nearly everybody had been
convinced that the Maginot Line was unassailable.

Now, the people of the northern half of France were stunned
by the strength and size of the German armed forces. In trucks
and tanks, on bikes and on foot, they swarmed everywhere,
penetrating into even the smallest, most isolated villages.

For the Ringot family Len's arrival meant, if only
symbolically, that all was not lost. It was another delusion, but
they had to cling to something and in helping Len they were
making a tiny gesture of fighting the all-conquering Germans.

As they sat in the cafe Len suggested that perhaps he should make for the south of France, even though this would be taking him further away from England. Desiré suggested that he go into hiding around Lille and wait for the inevitable British counter-attack. Neither he nor any other Frenchman then realised that after the defeat in France Britain had only one complete division to face the tremendous might of German's 150 divisions and practically no armour worth the name to fight Germany's new panzer divisions.

Len yielded to requests to stay a few days with Florentin and Zelfa but next day woke to bad news. The Germans had found one of their men dead with both hands severed at the wrists and they were demanding hostages. The mayor refused to give the names of ten young men so the Germans picked their own victims from town hall lists. These men would be shot, the Germans said, unless the culprit surrendered; and after that another ten and another ten until they had the guilty person in their hands. The situation looked grim until a German doctor realised that the dead man had died when a grenade exploded in his hands.

Len and Edouard went for a walk through the fields and came across a nauseating smell – the sickly, sweet and evil smell of putrefying human flesh. Tracing the odour to a cornfield they found fifteen crosses with a German helmet on each and nearby another grave on which hung a French helmet. A farmer came out and told them the story behind the graves. A Senegalese black soldier had refused to retreat with the rest of his company, insisting on staying behind to fight a lone rearguard action. He held out for twelve hours against overwhelming odds, delaying an entire company and killing fifteen Germans before himself being killed. The sixteen bodies had been laid out in a slight depression and covered with nothing more than a light layer of earth. In the heat vile putrefaction was inevitable.

Len and Edouard returned to Gondecourt and watched a German cavalry unit ride slowly through the town. As they stood in a doorway to let the impressive horsemen pass an elderly woman, Josephine Colot, held her forefinger and thumb to her nose and shouted to Len and the boy, 'My God, what a stink around here!' Then, as if surprised, she pointed a finger at the Germans. 'It must be them. The place really stinks of Boche.'

The officer leading the cavalry reined in and glared down at her. 'Be careful, madam,' he said tightly. 'Be very careful.' Mme Colot merely raised her eyebrows disdainfully and swept on with another twitch of her nostrils.

A few days later she gave Len a suit as another gesture of defiance against the Germans. Len stayed on with Zelfa and within days everybody in Gondecourt and for miles around knew about the escaped British soldier hiding in their midst. Watching Len cycle past, small children raised a clenched fist with thumb stuck upwards and shouted, 'O.K. Tommy!'

As a demonstration of defiance, affection and support it was magnificent but the townspeople's lack of understanding of basic security was lamentable. Once the busy Germans had time to organise their occupation both Len and the village would be terribly vulnerable. Florentin Ringot introduced Len to an elderly couple, Leonard and Marie Dhenin, who lived on the Wavrin road just out of Gondecourt, where they worked a farm with the help of their three daughters, Blanche 18, Florentine 35 and Marie-Sophie, 30, whose farmer husband was a prisoner of war.

The Dhenins asked Len if he would like to stay with them. Len had already weighed up the advantages of an isolated farm with open fields leading to woods and was happy to pay for hospitality by helping on the farm. Indeed, he was invaluable, being the only person who knew how to operate the threshing machine, formerly the function of Marie-Sophie's absent soldier-husband. During that August Len was busy and he felt reasonably safe; each evening he relaxed by going out with Paul, Marie-Sophie's eleven-year-old son, to set snares for rabbits.

Some French men and women were taking their first tentative steps in resistance to the Nazi occupation and one evening two young and intrepid girls from Annoeullin, Marcelle and Simone Brien, visited Len. They told him that they were members of a small group of people who had joined together to help shot-down airmen and escaped prisoners. Marcelle was the key person because she worked in the Social Security office and had access to documents and passes. She supplied Len with an authentic identity card in the name of Leonard Masseux of 8 Rue Nationale in Annoeullin, who was now dead. Len's photograph was fixed to the card and it looked official enough to fool German patrols. No French policeman would be taken in – especially as Len's command of French was crude – but the great majority of French were Anglophile and hated the Germans.

By now Len had met Adeline Cochet, a cousin of Zelfa Ringot, who told him that 'Madame Passy' was eager to meet him. She had been Jeanne Oliger – the name which appears on her memorial plaque – but everybody knew her as Madame Passy and held her in great respect. Len, while on leave in Britain early in 1940, had bought a record for her. She owned a country home but lived over her boutique in Gondecourt and Len met her in the kitchen. He was not easily awed by personalities but this tall, dignified and aristocratic widow was the type of woman for whom a soldier stood to attention. Graciously, she gestured to him to be seated and said in a formidable voice, 'We, the French people, will never accept the victory of the Nazis.'

'I'm sure you won't,' Len said. He knew from her tone and manner that she had declared personal war on the Germans.

'Can I count on your assistance, should I need it?' she asked.

'I'll do whatever you want me to do, Madame Passy,' Len promised. At that moment he had informally joined the Resistance, though he did not then know it.

His French was improving but as he was speaking mostly with farmers and mineworkers he was taking on the patois of northern France, which is distinctly different from formal French. Many people smiled when he spoke and Len could not understand why. They were merely amused to hear a foreigner speaking patois with all its idiosyncratic grammar and crude expletives. His French was quite good enough to read the warning notices posted by the German administration: Any civilian caught hiding enemy soldiers or airmen would be shot by firing squad. This was no idle threat, as the Nazis soon demonstrated, and Len became deeply worried about the people who were helping him.

One day a courier came to the Dhenin farm with a message that Madame Passy wished to see him. Around Gondecourt this was by now the equivalent of a royal command and Len hurried to obey. 'We have two escaped prisoners hiding in a gamekeeper's cottage,' she said, 'and I want you to certify that they are bona fide British.'

'Is there some doubt, Madame?' Len asked.

'There must always be doubt until we prove otherwise,' Madame Passy said crisply. 'It is up to you to find out if these men are what they say they are.' The embryo Resistance already knew that the Germans were infiltrating their own men, posing as evaders and escapers, into the rescue lines.

Len had met Monsieur Leon, Madame Passy's gamekeeper, and he cycled to his cottage in the woods. Leon showed him into a large room where a dozen people, including Marie-Sophie, were assembled. As Len took a chair from Leon and sat down a sudden silence fell, though Leon ended it with a laugh and everybody joined in. Two men, one of them aged about forty, looked about them, as if puzzled by the merriment and Len approached them. 'Are you two British?'

Both jumped to their feet and shook hands and the younger and larger man said, 'I'm George Young of the Grenadier Guards and this is Len Wilson from the Middlesex Regiment.'

Len was astounded. Len Wilson was from the same infantry company as himself and they had shared a barrack room at Gosport. More than that, he had sold Wilson an Echo radio for half a crown just before leaving Gosport for France. 'Len Wilson, eh?' Arlington said. 'Well Len, how's that radio I flogged you in Gosport last September?'

Wilson almost jumped off the floor in astonishment. 'Good God, Len Arlington!' he shouted. 'You look a right froggy in that outfit – I would never have recognised you.' He said that he and his mate had escaped three times and a great sense of relief came over everybody as Len vouched for the two men as

British. But everybody knew that the huge George Young, more than six feet six inches in height, would be singularly conspicuous and difficult to hide. This simple fact never did penetrate Young's own mind.

Marie-Sophie offered the use of her isolated and unoccupied farm as a hideout for the two men and Len, for his friends' safety, decided to join them. Marie-Sophie walked the mile or so with them, promised to bring food next day and left Len in charge. 'Just stay out of sight and you will be safe here,' she assured the soldiers.

Len slept well and was first up next morning. Cautiously exploring the vegetable garden he found nothing except some small carrots and turnips, and, hanging in the stables, some long strips of onions from which he made soup. Marie-Sophie arrived that afternoon to find three violently ill men collapsed on beds; Len's onions were garlic cloves and he had used fifty when one would have been ample. Later, while Young slept upstairs, Wilson swept the house and Len worked at the kitchen sink. Glancing casually through the window he was horrified to see a German staff car, with three immaculate officers, drive into the farmyard. Holding down instinctive fear, he hissed at Wilson, 'Watch out, Germans!' and sank beneath the level of the window. There seemed to be nothing menacing about the trio and he thought they would go away if their suspicions were not aroused.

He was too hopeful. Wilson pounded up the stairs and shouted 'Germans!' to Young. The big Grenadier awoke instantly, bent low and dived straight through the window. As it was shut tightly the crash was terrific and glass and timber flew everywhere. Young picked himself up, Wilson climbed out after him and both went haring across the fields.

Len, hearing the crash, swore at his departing comrades but kept his head and quietly pushed the outside door's barrel bolt into the locked position. Through the lace curtain he saw an officer approach the door and knock. He realised that from the other side of the house the Germans, incredibly, had not heard the smashing window or were ignoring it. Len stood stock still. The officer rattled the door knob, returned to the car and spoke to the others, and then they reversed and drove off. Len, already exasperated, spent two hours looking for Young and Wilson and had by then worked up an anger. He found them sitting against a haystack. 'You bloody fools!' he said. 'Don't you panic like that again or you'll be dead and so will I and God knows who else.' Young had not suffered as much as a scratch while making his spectacular dive.

That evening Len visited Florentin and Zelfa and found them excited; they had contacted a group on the other side of Lille who were supposedly organised by British Intelligence to assemble escaped prisoners and aircrew so that they could be flown back to England.

If this were so, the group was more advanced in its organisation and contacts than the Gondecourt cell. Len discussed the matter with Madame Passy, who had never heard of the group on the far side of the city. But, she said, it was worth contacting them, even at the risk of crossing Lille, especially as the newly heard of organisation was in the process of collecting a party of British.

Zelfa accompanied Len by bicycle while Young and Wilson, each with a French guide, travelled by train in separate compartments. Should any of the three escapers be stopped by police or Gestapo the French guide would go on as if a stranger to the Englishman. Len and Zelfa, some yards apart, were cycling across the bridge in the suburb of Fives when a man in a trilby hat and a raincoat stepped onto the road and signalled Len to stop. Zelfa did not keep to the pre-arranged plan and also stopped – a brave act of loyalty – but the man waved her on.

Holding out his hand, he said to Len, in French, 'Your identity card, please.' His language was clear but Len knew from his accent that he was German. He studied the card carefully. 'You live in Annoeullin?'

'Yes,' Len said with deliberate brevity.

The agent compared the card's photograph with Len in person and said, 'Très bien, merci.'

When Len caught up with Zelfa along the road she asked anxiously, 'Who was that?'

'German police, probably Gestapo,' Len said and Zelfa shuddered. Everybody feared the ruthless and thorough Gestapo agents, who seemed to be chosen for their lack of human feeling.

Their destination was a house in the Rue des Noirs, next to a baker's shop, and they were admitted by a stout woman, Madame Sangrez, who was about fifty. Rumour said that she had worked with the French secret service, the Deuxième Bureau, in World War 1 and was now helping British Intelligence. Young and Wilson had already arrived, as well as five other escaped British prisoners. Since there were only two bedrooms in the small house the men had to take turns to sleep. On the very first day time hung heavily on the men's hands and they frequently snapped at one another. They were young and accustomed to activity, and idleness unsettled them.

In an attempt to pass the time, Young, who had been a policeman in civilian life, organised mock court proceedings with Wilson as judge. Young played the reliable police witness, other men were the jury and the plaintiff was either Madame Sangrez or her teenage daughter. The charge was nearly always rape, which gave the men a chance to express their sexual repression and tension. As neither of the women understood English, the witnesses, called by Young and then incited by him, let their imagination run wild and all the sordid details were produced for the court.

The women, who were far from stupid, must have understood the substance of the mock trials but they tolerated them as they relieved the tension in the crowded house. One escaper was a highly nervous ginger-haired young Scot, whom Len saw as a menace to the rest of the party. He moaned and worried constantly and was clearly unstable. Late on the second day after the men had taken up residence, Madame Sangrez returned from a shopping trip looking even stouter than usual and when she took off her overcoat the soldiers saw that she had four revolvers tucked into her belt. When she laid them on the table Ginger picked one up and aimed it at Wilson and Young who were seated side by side on the settee. He pulled the trigger – and a bullet tore through the settee and embedded itself in the wall.

In the confined space the explosion was thunderous and, thinking quickly, Madame Sangrez hurried to the front door, where she joined other alarmed women in looking up and down the street in puzzlement. It was a beautiful piece of 'I-wonder-where-that-noise-came-from' play-acting.

Meanwhile Young had grabbed Ginger by the throat. 'You stupid bastard, what did you do that for?' he growled angrily, and flung down the Scot when he muttered that he had not expected the revolver to be loaded.

After three weeks virtual imprisonment, late one night Len followed Madame Sangrez into her back garden. She was standing against a wall and peering upwards and waiting for a signal, she said. Intrigued, Len waited with her and about midnight they heard an aircraft engine. A searchlight probed the sky and at once the plane dropped three flares – red, white, red.

At that time, late in 1940, the German anti-aircraft and searchlight teams challenged planes in this way. The code was changed each night so that the gunners would know at once whether a plane was friendly or hostile. Since they did not open fire on this occasion the plane was obviously German, nevertheless Madame Sangrez said, 'That's the signal; the British will be coming for you tomorrow night.'

Len was startled and worried. 'But that was a German plane,' he said.

Mme Sangrez was annoyed at being questioned and Len's danger-sensing nerve began to twitch. The woman was a German agent or she was stupid or she did not know the correct signals. In any case the situation was dangerous for the men in her house. He called Young and Wilson into conference in a corner of the hall. 'Something funny is going on,' he said softly, 'and I'm all for clearing out tomorrow – back to Gondecourt. But not a word to anybody else.'

For Madame Sangrez they concocted a story that they were heading for the French coast and the woman raised no objection. They set off early next morning, Len leading on his

bike and waiting at each crossroad where it was necessary to
make a turn until Young and Wilson had sighted him and knew
the way. In this way he guided them out of Lille. Clear of the
town, he left the other two under cover behind a shed and
cycled to Marie-Sophie's farm. This journey took him fifteeen
minutes and the return trip fifteen minutes. In that half-hour
Young and Wilson had disappeared. After a quick and fruitless
search on the outskirts of Lille, Len hurried back to the farm,
half expecting that the pair had played a joke on him and that
he would find them there. Marie-Sophie, her sister Florentine
and Paul took their bikes and scoured the countryside. By now
they had a real fear that a German patrol had picked up the two
men and that meant danger, for Len doubted if either Young or
Wilson could keep their mouths shut.

For the rest of the day everybody at the farm was worried and
miserable and hourly expecting trouble. Desiré Ringot brought
news of that trouble – Young and Wilson were in the Cafe Mayeur
in Gondecourt, both were drunk and they were singing at the
top of their voices. And, as if that were not bad enough, the cafe
was full of German troops who were also very drunk and
singing. Aghast, Len and Marie-Sophie raced to their bikes and
pedalled madly for Gondecourt. They pulled up outside the cafe
and Len was horrified to hear two British voices bawling 'It's a long
way to Tipperary'. Worse, fifty German voices were also singing the
song – in German. The tune, though with different words, was as
well known to them as Lili Marlene became to the British. In the
fearful uproar the Nazis had not noticed that two 'French
civilians' were singing in English.

'I'm going in,' Len said grimly and put out a hand to
stop Marie-Sophie but she ignored the gesture and entered with
him. Almost at once Len knew that this move had been a mistake;
if Young and Wilson saw him they would shout at him in English
and the Germans, no matter how drunk, would understand. He
signalled to Marie-Sophie and they sidled out of the cafe.

'There's only one way to do this,' Len said to the French woman.
'You pretend to be George Young's wife and you are very annoyed
at the state he's in. Go in there, clout him around the ears and drag

him out by the scruff of the neck before he can say anything.' He did not stop to think that to grab the giant Grenadier by the scruff of the neck Marie-Sophie would have to stand on a ladder.

The courageous Marie-Sophie did not hesitate. Pushing her way into the crowded cafe she shoved German soldiers aside and, talking non-stop, reached Young. 'You drunken pig!' she screamed. 'You stupid oaf, you are supposed to be shovelling up cow dung and I find you here. You're a great lump of dung yourself, you imbecile . . .' Young did not understand a word of this but the fury of the tirade startled him and several times he tried to say somthing. Each time Marie-Sophie jumped up and hit him across the mouth or kicked his shins. She also found time to swear furiously at the more meek Wilson whenever he seemed likely to speak. As she pushed Young towards the door through the crowd of Germans they laughed uproariously and cheered her. And it really was funny to see a little woman bullying a giant of a man. Len Wilson, also overwhelmed by Marie-Sophie's assault, followed passively behind her. As the trio disappeared the German soldiers gave a final cheer.

Len met them around the corner and he and Marie-Sophie cajoled and harried the two men back to the farm, afraid all the time that someone among the Germans would suddenly realise that he had been listening to an English song and raise the alarm. Young and Wilson slept off their stupor that night and next day Len and the others heard what had happened. A brewer's van driver had picked them up where Len had left them and they had cheerfully told him they were British soldiers. He was so pleased that he insisted in stopping for a drink at every cafe on the way to Gondecourt. Finally he had taken them into the Cafe Mayeur but when he saw the place packed with Germans he had quickly left, leaving Young and Wilson to enjoy a last drink with the Germans. Other Frenchmen in the cafe, including the proprietor, knew what was happening but dared not speak to the English soldiers. Finally, somebody had slipped out and told Desiré Ringot.

Len was by now terrified of the dangers to which the thoughtless Young and Wilson were exposing his French friends. When the pair announced a few days later that they were going to make for Free France – in the south – he did not try too hard to dissuade them. They said goodbye one afternoon and walked briskly away but word soon reached Len that they had been spotted on the road leading to the Belgian frontier – that is, they were heading north instead of south. Exasperated by such stupidity, Len raced after them on his bike to put them on the right road. 'God Almighty!' he shouted when he had cut them off. 'Don't you know that you're heading due north?'

'Are we?' George Young said and turned to Wilson. 'Did you know that Len?'

'Buggered if I did,' Wilson confessed.

Len got them turned around, said goodbye again, watched them walk off then sat on his bike and shook his head. 'They'll never make it,' he said to himself. He only hoped that they would travel a long distance before they were picked up and that by then they would have forgotten that such a place as Gondecourt had ever existed.

In September of 1940 another escaped prisoner of war, a Scot named Sergeant Major Alex Keiller, came to visit Len at the Dhenin's farm in Gondecourt. He was hiding in Allennes-les-Marais, about four kilometres from Gondecourt. From the moment of meeting Len distrusted Keiller and decided to be very wary. With a great show of secrecy, Keiller showed him a small revolver which he said he always carried.

'What do you want that for?' Len asked.

'They'll never take me alive,' Keiller said grimly.

'Look,' Len said patiently. 'If you do get caught and the Germans find that gun on you they will certainly torture you. And they'll go on doing it until you give them the name of every French person who has helped you.'

Grandpère Dhenin, who had heard Keiller and Len talking, said after he had gone, 'I don't trust that fellow.'

'There's something strange about him,' Len agreed. 'Something odd.'

That same evening Zelfa Ringot's cousin, Adeline Cochet, visited Zelfa's home. She wanted Len to meet her brother, Pierre Faucomprez, who lived in the nearby village of Chemy, which had only 300 inhabitants. The heavily moustached Faucomprez, a tall and thin but tough farm worker, welcomed Len warmly, as did his wife Sophie, known as Fi-Fi, and their daughters, Jervaise, eighteen, and Marcelle, thirteen. Len took to the cheerful, friendly family at once. As he and Adeline were about to set off to return to Gondecourt, Pierre and Fi-Fi told him that he could use their home as a hideout at any time, should Gondecourt become too dangerous.

Such an offer was priceless and Len appreciated the cold courage and warm hearts it represented. Back in Gondecourt, Edouard hurried in to Len to say that two British escaped prisoners were hiding in the coal town of Billy-Berclau, about ten miles away. Len at once thought of Young and Wilson and sighed, 'They didn't get far, did they?' he said wearily. He and Edouard were in Billy-Berclau by 8.30 next morning and stopped at a cafe on a corner of the town square, whose owner was a Resistance man. After the usual discreet question and answer to establish identity, the cafe owner took Len and Edouard to a farm.

Here the met the two escapers – not Young and Wilson – but Stan Golding from Longheath, near Croydon, and Bill Jackson, known as Jack, from Sheffield. Stan was a corporal and Jack a driver with the Royal Army Service Corps. They had escaped from a column of prisoners near Tournai, Belgium, and they had exchanged their army uniforms for clothes stolen from farm washing lines. Jack was a fair-haired young man, a year older than Len, while Stan was a few years older still. He was already starting to become stout and looked older than his years; Len thought he was about thirty-five.

Len was startled to see that Stan wore spats, hardly an ideal sartorial adornment for a man trying to avoid being noticed. Delighted to meet Len, Stan wanted to celebrate and insisted on standing drinks at a cafe near a small chateau, midway between Billy and Berclau. 'Don't you think it's dangerous drinking in cafes so close to your hideout?' Len asked worriedly.

'Hell no,' Stan said. 'Everybody around here knows us and they're only too pleased to see us. Anyway, our place is at Haisnes, about five miles away.'

The middle-aged woman who owned the cafe served the small party with genièvre, a crude gin, and coal miners who came in later plied the escapers with other drinks.

The liquor seduced Len from his sense of caution and duty and he did not take enough care of Edouard, who was unused to alcohol and became violently ill. As he had promised to visit Madame Passy, he left Edouard asleep in some straw in the cafe's outhouse and returned to Gondecourt, where Zelfa sharply scolded him for leaving her son. Then she forced him to return to Billy-Berclau and rescue Edouard.

The following week Len again met Stan and Jack in their favourite cafe in Billy-Berclau and they insisted that he come with them to Haisnes to meet the people who were hiding them. Not that these two spent much time hiding. Neither had learnt any French, they spoke openly in English and wherever they went they were known. Most dangerous of all, in this region lived many foreign workers, including Poles and Italians who might easily be induced to denounce escapers.

Stan and Jack lived with Monsieur Durbureaux, a retired coal miner of about sixty, his crippled wife and their schoolgirl daughter, Huguette, about eighteen years of age. Having exhibited Len to the Dubureaux family, Stan and Jack took him to the Cafe Leignel. By now Len was very uneasy for he felt that these two were not only a danger to themselves but to others.

Len had a proprietorial interest in the region and liked to know what was going on – and Madame Passy valued the information he brought. People trusted him too and when next he visited Haisnes he dropped in on M. Leignel in his cafe. After some hesitation, the Frenchman swore Len to secrecy and asked for his help. He was a member of a group that had organised itself to sabotage the local chemical factory, Finalens, but the group was worried about the presence of Stan and Jack; if they were to be caught the Gestapo would comb through the area with ruthless efficiency. The Dubureaux's house was only fifty yards from the factory entrance so the Gestapo would give it particular attention.

'So how can I help?' Len asked.

'You must persuade your friends to move from the factory area. Find them another place to hide.'

Len thought that inducing Stan and Jack to move from their comfortable hideout might be difficult and when he hesitated Leignel said, 'Come and talk it over with one of my friends.'

They walked to the home of Victor Dejong, a director in the Finalens firm. A tall, pleasant and intelligent looking man, Dejong and his attractive wife – Len was fascinated by her long platinum hair – were key figures in local Resistance. He, too, said that a safer place had to be found for Stan and Jack and undertook to look for one. 'Come back in a week's time,' he told Len.

The local people had been quick to notice that Len was cautious and security-conscious and they put a great deal of trust in him.

Back in his own territory, Len called on Pierre and Fi-Fi Faucomprez who were about to visit some friends in Fives. Len accompanied them just to see the house in Rue des Noirs and find out about Madame Sangrez's operation. He and Fi-Fi Faucomprez made a reconnaissance and the moment they turned into the Rue des Noirs two men in raincoats and trilby hats stared insolently at them. This outfit was rare in northern France and again Len sensed danger. The shutters over the windows of the Sangrez house had been smashed in so Fi-Fi and Len walked past with only a casual glance and knocked on the door of the bakery next door.

The elderly man who opened the door was covered with flour. Recognising Len, he said in a gasp, 'Entrez, vite!' As he closed the door he said fearfully, 'You didn't knock next door, did you? No? Thank God for that! Those men at the end of the street are arresting every person who knocks at the door.'

Len's anticipation of danger had been justified. The other British escapers had also left the Sangrez house and the Gestapo pounced soon after this, arresting Madame Sangrez and her daugher. Both women were sent to a concentration camp and disappeared for ever.

8

A Lady of the Resistance

Christmas, 1940, was approaching. The French were about to 'celebrate' their first Christmas under occupation and they knew now that deliverance was a long way off. The might of Germany and the inability of Britain to mount a counter-offensive was all to obvious. Len, visiting Berclau again, met Stan – who was now trying to get people to call him François – and had a few too many drinks with him. When he returned to the Faucomprez home at Chemy he was unsteady on his feet and Fi-Fi cooked him some eggs and chips. Then she set his meal on the green and white oilcloth of the kitchen table and stood with her back to the hot stove. As Len ate, Fi-Fi gossiped cheerfully and warned Len about the perils of French liquor.

Suddenly she was silent and Len looked up from his plate to see this calm and happy person transfixed with horror as she looked through the glass of the kitchen door. The door flew open and three German officers entered. The leader, noticing her terror, said sharply, 'What are you afraid of Madame?'

Fi-Fi pulled herself together. 'We are not used to soldiers bursting into our home like that,' she said.

The German smiled. 'We have been knocking but had no answer, so we came in. The door was not locked.' He glanced at Len who went on eating his eggs and chips though his throat was so tight with tension that he nearly choked. 'Who is this man?'

'He is my son,' Fi-Fi said. 'He is going night work.'

From that moment the officers completely ignored Len. The leader explained that they were seeking billets for 600 men who would be stationed in Chemy for a time. Her house was out of the question as a billet, Fi-Fi said; her son had one bedroom while she and her husband shared the other with their two daughters.

The inspecting officers found the small room adjoining the narrow passage near the front door, used by the Faucomprez family as a storeroom and for their boxes. 'This will be suitable for six men,' the spokesman said. 'They will arrive tonight. They will bring their own mattresses and sleep on the floor.'

'In this weather!' Fi-Fi objected. 'There's not even a fireplace.'

'We will arrange for a stove to be fitted,' the officer said irritably. 'Every morning you will provide hot coffee for the six men and each will pay you five francs. I trust you have no more objections, Madame!' And they marched out.

Fi-Fi and Len sighed with relief but Len said sadly, 'Well, that's that, I'll have to leave before they arrive. It will be much too dangerous for you with six Germans in the house.'

Fi-Fi was thoughtful. 'Don't be hasty. It's not actually written on your face that you are British. Provided that none of the Germans speak French you will be quite safe.'

For a week of winter 1940 Len slept soundly upstairs while six Nazi stormtroopers slept below, effectively protecting him. Every day they left at 8 a.m., never returning before 6 p.m.

Len kept his appointment in Berclau with Victor Dejong, the Dutchman who was a member of the local Resistance group. Dejong, who worked in the town hall at Douvrin, had obtained an identity card for Len in the name of Maurice Manessier, born at Carvin in the Calais Département on September 12, 1921. As Len often crossed from the Nord Départment to Calais district he needed an identity pass for each so he was grateful to the helpful Dejong.

That evening Dejong took him to a Resistance meeting in the town hall – of all places – where he met M. Andrieux, whose wife was a schoolteacher. Every member of the group was worried about the lack of security, especially about the risks which Stan and Jack were taking. Andrieux had found an isolated house owned by a widow, who would take them in provided that they did not show themselves. It was Len's job to convince the two soldiers of their danger. He found them in their usual happy-go-lucky frame of mind and spoke to them bluntly. 'You can't last here very long. It's only a matter of time before you are caught. When that happens you will probably be treated as prisoners of war but your French friends will be tortured for weeks and in the end they'll be shot. It's your duty to protect these people from unnecessary risks.'

The two men were reluctant to move but finally Jack said, 'O.K., provided that we can return and see Mr and Mrs Dubureaux.'

'For God's sake, no!' Len said. 'That would be like pointing a rifle at them. You two have to remain in hiding while friends of mine try to arrange your return to England.'

Len was insistent and got the pair out of the Dubureaux's house that evening. The new hideout was about four miles away and the only transport was his bike; Len put Jack, who was the smallest, on the handlebars while Stan rode on the luggage carrier. 'Right,' he said, 'now if there's any trouble, don't panic. Sit tight and leave any talking to me.' He was already framing a story that he was taking two drunken friends home from a cafe.

He had pedalled nearly to Billy when a German road patrol of an officer and ten men loomed in front of them. Even before Len could properly brake, Stan and Jack leapt off the bike in wild panic and raced off into the darkness of the fields. The officer stared after them, perplexed, then pushed his helmet back and scratched his head in puzzlement. 'Papers, please,' he ordered Len and then he closely examined the identity card, flashing his torch into Len's face. Handing it back, he stared again in the direction taken by the other two and muttered in German. Len helped him out by tapping his own forehead, as if to say that his friends were feeble-minded. In fact, he was glad they had taken off; their lack of papers would have been hard to explain.

The German nodded and ordered his patrol forward, leaving Len alone. Whistling the *Beer Barrel Polka*, Len cycled about 300 yards and Stan and Jack appeared by the roadside. The arrangement was for the escapers to enter a cafe owned by Madame Morand, who would take them to the hideout. As he reached this cafe Len said, 'Right you two go in while I find a place for the bike.'

This took only a few seconds and as he entered the cafe two charging men knocked him flying down the steps. Angry, confused and alarmed he looked up from the ground to see Stan and Jack again running in mad panic. Curious, he entered the cafe, dusting himself off, and saw two German officers in shirt-sleeves staring at him suspiciously over their glasses of beer. Retreat would have been disastrous so Len advanced to the bar and cocking his thumb in the direction of the door, he said. 'Those two must be completely bonkers.'

The officers did not understand his patois ('Ils sont complètement maboule, ces deux là') and shrugged. Len tapped finger to forehead and repated 'Maboule'.

They smiled at that and went on with their drinking while Len ordered a drink for himself. After ten minutes the Germans left the cafe and Len called Madame Morand, to whom he gave the password provided by M. Andrieux, as well as a note from him. The women read it and eyed him in amazement. 'You are English and you have the nerve to stand there drinking next to German officers!'

'My friends left me no option,' Len said rather sourly. 'And now I had better look for them.' He found Stan and Jack in another cafe, which was also a cycle repair shop, and gave them a sharp lecture on the need for self-control. He returned them to Madame Morand and was relieved when she said that she would take them to the safe house, about 600 metres directly behind her cafe and in the woods. Len could go home.

Returning to Chemy, Len heard from Fi-Fi that Madame Passy needed him urgently and Len obeyed this summons next morning. He walked into the Gondecourt boutique to find five German officers in heated argument over prices with her daugher Yvonne. The girl was only sixteen but she handled the situation posed by Len's arrived with great coolness. 'Ah, Leonard,' she said, 'mother is in the kitchen waiting for you.'

With a shop full of Nazis, Len and Madame Passy sat a few feet away in her kitchen while they discussed Resistance affairs.

It was an exquisite situation and they both enjoyed it. 'I am pleased that you came so quickly, Leonard,' Madame said. In French the name has three syllables – Lee/on/ar(d) – and Len had become accustomed to hearing it pronounced that way. One of our group has a man in hiding. He says he is a Royal Air Force pilot who was shot down in Belgium. Will you talk with him discreetly and find out if he really is a British pilot?'

Yvonne, having got rid of the German officers, guided Len to the house, which was on the outskirts of Gondecourt. Inside Len was introduced to the pilot and at once distrusted him. A slight, dark-haired, young man, he spoke perfect English but to Len's critical eye he did not look the part. The man was unaware that Len was, in effect, vetting him, for he went about his job with a conversational ease that many a professional interrogator would have envied.

'Well, you've been lucky so far,' Len said, settling himself comfortably in a chair.

'I suppose I have,' the pilot admitted, 'though I didn't feel lucky when I bailed out.'

'You know, I almost joined the RAF before the war,' Len said. 'Flying must be blooming well better than walking any day! How did you get shot down?'

'I was attacked by a Messerschmidt 109 but I managed to get off a burst of cannon fire at him at the same time,' the flier said. 'So although I had to bail out, the Messerschmidt also went down in flames.'

'You were flying a Spitfire?' Len said.

'Oh no, a Hurricane.'

This answer told Len that there was something 'funny' about the flier. Len knew his aircraft – and at that point in the war no British fighter planes had cannon mounted on them; Spitfires and Hurricanes carried eight machine guns mounted on their wings. (The first cannon were mounted on Spitfires at the end of 1941). He was worried; he held this man's life in his hands. The flier seemed a little tense so to put him more at ease Len described his escape after Dunkirk. 'We were to be picked up by plane at that time,' he said, 'and now I'm probably going back to England on the same plane as you. I'm told that it will be a Westland Lysander. Is that a very big plane?'

'Oh fairly big,' the flier said. 'It's a single-seater biplane.'

Len feigned some heavy thought. 'Suppose it is attacked by German night fighters? Can it defend itself?'

'Certainly,' the other man said. 'It has four heavy machine guns and it's very manoeuvrable – more than a match for any Messerschmidt.'

Len no longer had any doubt; this man was no RAF pilot but a German agent planted on the escape line. There were holes in his aviation knowledge. The Lysander was not a big plane but only a two-seater and it was a monoplane, not a biplane. It did have four machine guns – though not 'heavy' ones – and at 237 mph it was no match for the current Messerschmidt, which flew at well over 300 mph.

After a while Len said, 'Well, I'll come back tomorrow with details of our escape.'

To Madame Passy he said, 'This man may not be German but he's in their service and he's dangerous. How can we get rid of him?'

'We can arrange that tonight,' the grand lady said with quiet finality. 'I have a group of men who will take any step necessary to keep our operation secure. We can safely leave the matter in their hands.'

In effect, Len had pronounced the man's death sentence and he was never again seen in Gondecourt – nor was he spoken of. He was a casualty in a necessarily ruthless war.

It was important that Len should be known to all the villagers so that they would not, in the wrong company, express surprise at his presence. One evening Fi-Fi and Marcelle took him to meet Jerome Bulcourt, a 60-year-old widower who had brought up alone his two daughters, Marthe, 21, and Charline, 17. It was a pleasant evening and Len liked the peaceful, homely atmosphere. Jerome, a rugged, contented farmer, sat in an old armchair before a roaring fire with a large beer. Several times he took a red-hot poker from the fire and plunged it into the beer glass, which he then drained.

That evening Marthe was visited by her fiancé, Louis Bonte, a well built man of twenty-six with a bold, confident manner. When Len was introduced as an escaped prisoner of war Louis crushed his fingers in a handshake of exuberant goodwill. It was arranged that at Marthe's wedding reception in a week's time Len would be introduced as the Faucomprezs' cousin from Belgium. The friendly Louis invited him, next day, to Dom-Sainghin where his mother was housekeeper in a large chateau, whose owners had gone to live in unoccupied France. Madame Bont offered Len a safe bedroom any time he needed it.

The Bulcourt-Bonte wedding reception was held in a hall near Chemy village church and was a bright and happy occasion, with the occupation temporarily forgotten. Wine flowed freely and the music and singing became very noisy. At eleven p.m. the war returned – four German military policemen burst through the doors and shouted for silence. Their leader said, 'This is an identity paper check. Everybody will be seated and prepare their papers for inspection.' Two of the Germans stood in the middle of the hall with their machine pistols at the ready while the others started to examine papers.

Len kept his head but was dismayed. He had no papers with him. The door was thirty yards away and he had no chance of surviving a dash for freedom. He considered sidling to the far end of the hall and slipping through a window but the police were constantly vigilant. 'Len lad,' he said ruefully to himself, 'You've had it this time.' But then he caught the eye of Jerome Bulcourt, who winked at him. As host, Bulcourt took a tray of champagne glasses to the Germans and explained that they had come into a wedding party. Would they care to drink to the health of the bride and groom? After some hesitation the leader took a glass and the others followed. Then they threw their glasses into a corner, where they smashed. This was a German wedding custom, they said, and some of the guests cheered. Bulcourt pressed more champagne on them and as it was difficult to hold two glasses of champagne and a Schmeisser the firearms were holstered. When a crowd of guests screened the Germans Len, Fi-Fi and Marcelle slipped through the door.

Len became friendly with Louis and Marthe and often visited them; he liked to discuss the war with Louis who seemed to have an intelligent grasp of its larger issues. He also took advantage of Madame Bonte's invitation to stay at the chateau, where the old woman treated him as she would her own son. In the big isolated chateau Len experienced a degree of security that just did not exist in the villages and towns.

The six Germans in Fi-Fi's house had given no trouble. Not that this made them any more acceptable to the villagers, who did all they could to annoy the Germans. At Christmas the six got drunk in the front room and then went out into the freezing cold to throw buckets of water over one another. Two joined the family, including Len, in the kitchen and offered cigars, which were declined. The Faucomprez family, like the vast majority of families affected by the occupation, gave the Germans no opportunity to become friendly, though Len asked one of them for his address, thinking that after the war it might be fun to tell him that he had shared a billet with a British Tommy. In the second week of January the German unit was withdrawn from Chemy and nobody was sorry to see them go.

As promised, Len returned to Berclau about the end of January to see Stan and Jack, only to be told by Mme Morand that they had disappeared. Len sensed at once that they had returned to the Dubureaux home and he hurried to the house. As he leaned his bike against the wall he heard Mme Dubureaux call out, 'Quick, Stan and Jack, hide! It's Leonard.'

She even tried to deceive Len, by asking as she met him at the door, 'Hullo, Len, how are Stan and Jack?'

Len whispered in her ear, 'Quick, Stan and Jack, hide, here's Leonard.'

She took this in good grace and called the pair from hiding. Stan rather petulantly said, 'Look here, Len, we had to come back. That old woman in Berclau never spoke a word to us all day. We really got browned off there.'

Len tried to talk sense into them and they promised to return to Berclau after a while. Len could only unhappily leave the situation like that. A sinister and very able Gestapo agent had come into the district and his presence was worrying nearly everybody who had any secrets involving Resistance work or help to the British. A little man, he was known as Bruno, and he had the appearance and the persistence of a ferret. Len had caught a glimpse of the man and he knew at once that he was dangerous – the type of man who would enjoy the hunt for 'terrorists' and 'traitors'.

In the villages the greatest risk was at night for that was when the Gestapo planned its raids but during the day there was another kind of risk in the streets of the big towns – that of being recognised by somebody who might inadvertently draw the attention of a German patrol or a passing Gestapo pimp. Len went to Lille one day to check out, with a new group he had heard of, the possibility of getting back to Britain. In the Rue de Bethune, with his thoughts on England, he was startled to hear 'Bonjour Leonard!' The caller was Eugenie Hochart, whose parents owned a butcher's shop in Annoeullin; parents and daughter had been arrested for hiding a British escaped prisoner. Now here she was in Lille. And that was not all. She was escorted by a German soldier. 'I have a toothache,' Eugenie told Len, 'and I've been allowed out of prison to visit a dentist.'

'I understand,' Len said cautiously. He thought the less he said the better.

Eugenie turned to the soldier. 'This is my cousin. You understand?'

The German nodded and held out his hand. Len shook it and wondered wrily if this act could be interpreted as collaboration with the enemy. Characteristically, he played the bluff to the limit and pointing to a nearby cafe he pantomimed an offer of a drink of beer. The three sat at a table for fifteen minutes, while Eugenie told Len of conditions in Loos prison. The German's French was poor so he understood little of this; he was content enough with his beer. After a time he grunted 'Schnell!' and the fraternising was over. At that time Eugenie and her mother had not been tried; a few weeks later both were sentenced to four years in the prison.

Len had yet another shock that day. Making for the Fives

district, he entered the Rue Faidherbe and saw an SS man approaching. He was a solidly built soldier, fully equipped with greatcoat, steel helmet, rifle and full marching kit. A split second after he had passed the SS man Len felt a powerful slap on the shoulder and thought momentarily that he was in for a fight. Instead, the SS man said pleasantly in French, 'Well, Leonard, don't you say hello to your friends?'

Len was shocked almost dumb. The SS man was Louis Bonte. Disbelievingly, he said, 'You're wearing SS uniform!'

Bonte winked at him. 'Intelligence service,' he said enigmatically. And when Len was still silent he added, 'Don't be afraid, there's no danger. See you soon.'

He shook hands with Len and marched off, leaving Len bewildered. Bonte had enlisted in the Waffen SS, though none of his friends knew why. His mother collapsed when he turned up at home in German uniform and died a few days later; nobody had any doubt that her heart was broken.

After service on the Russian front, Bonte was sent to France on leave. He was not, of course, on any 'intelligence service' and by now he realised what a terrible mistake he had made, and he deserted. If he expected his former French friends to be sympathetic and shelter him he was tragically mistaken. One act of treachery was enough to damn a man for life; Louis Bonte had committed an even greater crime – he had donned the hated enemy uniform and fought against allies of France. Somebody denounced him to the German authorities and he was caught. Quickly court-martialled, he was executed by firing squad. Not even his widow mourned him, and if she knew why he had done such a mad thing she never revealed it, not even to Len.

For some months in the first half of 1941 life was blessedly uneventful, though Len was generally busy with Resistance matters, and he spent much of his time cultivating his contacts in the Lille district. He had a feeling that he would be needing friends and safe houses. Despite his problems and apprehensions Len was feeling fairly secure at this time. He and Marcelle even ran the risk of having their photograph taken together – and it was a risk even when the photographer was

Adeline Cochet's son. The Gestapo always looked for incriminating photographs when they searched suspect houses. Marcelle was looking darkly pretty as she sat upright in a chair, with Len half turned towards her. As fair-haired as Marcelle was dark, he was smiling and his wide-set eyes were trouble-free. The very pose suggested a growing intimacy between the young French girl and the soldier in disguise, and the photographer coaxed Len into putting an arm around Marcelle.

About this time Jack and Stan (or François as he was at the time) turned up at the Faucomprez house in Chemy to visit Len, who was out on a Resistance errand. During the afternoon Fi-Fi had to visit a farmer on the other side of the village, so Jack and Stan accompanied her. On the way they passed a cherry orchard with the trees laden with fruit. Unable to resist the temptation, they climbed the fence and helped themselves. Fi-Fi tried to explain that a German officer was billeted in the house at the back of the orchard but they took no notice. She walked on so as not to be in immediate danger should the men get caught. After a time they caught up with her and presented her with some cherries. Fi-Fi was too courteous to tell the men that they had taken an unwarrantable risk, not only with their own lives but with hers. When Len heard about the incident later he was more outspoken. Jack and Stan had risked his neck too. 'My God!' he said to Fi-Fi. 'Can you imagine what would have happened if that Boche officer had seen them at the cherries?' She and Len discussed the incident and she advised Len not to encourage the other Englishmen to come to Chemy. 'We have friends who give us cherries,' she said, 'it is foolish to steal from the Germans.'

That summer a stranger arrived in Gondecourt, and he told everybody who cared to listen that he was a British Intelligence officer, code-named Joe – though Len heard that he sometimes used the name Francis Mumme. He had been wounded, he said, in a shoot-out with Gestapo agents. In sympathy the Lehoucq family took him in and on the first morning, after the young housewife had taken him a cup of coffee in his bedroom, he asked her if she would massage him as his wound was painful He pulled back the bedclothes and she saw that he was naked;

nevertheless she massaged him without seeing any wound. Then, to her surprise, he asked her for six eggs for breakfast; in England, he said, he always breakfasted on a dozen eggs.

Len, who was passed all this information along the Resistance network, was profoundly uneasy. It seemed to him inconceivable that a British agent would so readily identify himself in a region crawling with Gestapo agents and army police. One morning, while he was helping Pierre Faucomprez on his allotment, Joe knocked next door and told the neighbour, Madame Duhem, 'I am a friend of Leonard, the Englishman. He asked me to call on him today but I'm not sure where he is staying. He is with you, perhaps?'

The unsuspecting Mme Duhem said, 'Oh, no, he's with the Faucomprezs next door.'

Len had seen Joe's arrival but had not heard this conversation. To Pierre he said, 'I don't like the look of that man; he's got Boche written all over him.'

Fi-Fi came hurrying into the garden. 'Quick Len, hide!' she said urgently. 'There's a man asking for you and I don't like the look of him.'

Len vanished into the fields while Pierre got rid of Joe but he too sensed 'something queer' about the man. Len had nightmares that night of the house being surrounded by Germans and all of them being captured. Next day he did what common sense demanded – he reported the matter to Madame Passy, who was already worried by the stranger's presence. Len characteristically decided that it was up to him to take action; he would visit Joe and check him out. He had been accompanied from Gondecourt by the Faucomprez dog, a bitch called Tommy who had an amazing natural aversion to Germans. She would attack any German who happened to be passing and for her own safety had to be restrained. Now she went with Len to the big Lehoucq house, where he spoke to Madame Lehoucq. 'Word reached me yesterday that a British officer was looking for me in Chemy,' he said, 'so I have come to see him.'

The woman was dubious. 'He's rather annoyed. He went out of his way to see you yesterday and you wouldn't show yourself. But I will ask him.' She left the kitchen and Len heard her climbing the wooden stairs to the bedrooms. Tommy's neck hairs bristled and she growled angrily, always a sign that Germans were about. Mme Lehoucq returned and said curtly, 'He refuses to see you.'

'Then maybe I'll see him,' Len said, jumping up and making for the stairs.

The woman called, 'Whatever happens, I will not be responsible!'

Tommy arrived at the top of the stairs before Len and sniffed at each door along the passage, finally stopping to growl at the fourth one. 'That's Joe's room, Leonard,' said José, Mme Lehoucq's daughter, who had appeared.

Len stepped quickly inside, surprising a man lying in a large double bed – though it was now past eleven a.m. As he tried to struggle into a sitting position and to slide a hand under his pillow Tommy sprang onto his stomach and her teeth snapped viciously only inches from his face.

'Get this damned animal off me!' he shouted.

'Just lie still and don't move,' Len said, 'and she won't harm you.' He took a long careful look at Joe. He was about thirty-five and powerfully built, with hair receding rapidly from his forehead, and he looked unpleasant and formidable. He had been drinking heavily the evening before and his hangover shakes were obvious.

'I hear that you were looking for me yesterday in Chemy,' Len said, still standing.

'Don't talk in English!' Joe said. 'Somebody might overhear us.'

'What does that matter? Don't you trust Madame Lehoucq and her family?'

'Of course I do but you never know who else might be listening.' As he moved in the bed Tommy nearly took his nose between her snapping teeth. 'Take this bloody dog off me, I can't move!'

Len ignored his plea and said again, this time in French, 'You were looking for me in Chemy yesterday.'

'Yes! And that damned woman lied and said she didn't know you.'

Len was intent on drawing attention away from the Faucomprez house, so he said casually, 'I don't know where you went but I'm pretty certain that whoever you spoke to probably never had heard of me. She would be telling the truth.'

'But the woman next door insisted that it was the right house, your house.'

'Just where in Chemy was this house?' When Joe described the whereabouts of the Faucomprez home, Len said, 'Ah, you spoke to Madame Duhem, I think. She's a mental case. You went to the wrong house. I'm staying with people on the other side of Chemy, near the chateau.'

Joe let that pass. 'I have orders from London to arrange your return to England.'

'And how are you going to manage that?'

'You can come with me. I'm leaving this afternoon and that's my case ready packed.' He pointed to a small suitcase.

'No, I'm not ready to go,' Len said. 'I'm safe here for the moment and I don't have to take orders from anybody.'

With an air of authority, Joe said, 'I shall have to report to London that you refused to take my orders.'

'You do that. Tell them in London that I will carry on here.'

Joe changed the subject. 'Do you know Alex Keiller, the Scotsman?'

'I've heard of him. Why?'

'He's a friend of mine,' Joe said. 'He's staying with some people in Allens.'

'That I don't know, as I have never been to see him.'

But Len thought it was significant that Joe knew Keiller; it had to mean that they were in league and therefore both were enemy agents. 'Well, cheerio for now,' he said. 'See you in London one day.' He called Tommy off the bed and was quickly through the door. Len wanted to get out of the house quickly but he stopped to warn Mme Lehoucq. 'Now you have something to be responsible for,' he said grimly, throwing her words back at her. 'That man up there is a Gestapo agent and you will have to get rid of him as quickly as possible.' He left the woman looking pale and frightened.

Len gave Madame Passy the same report and she looked frowning seriously. 'Something drastic will have to be done about him then. Are you quite sure he's not a British agent?'

'There's absolutely nothing British about him,' Len assured her. He reasoned that if Joe really was a British officer – and he already knew that Len was a British soldier – his approach would have been much more officer-to-man. Apart from all the other suspicious signs, Len was relying on Tommy's hunch; this extraordinary dog was never wrong about Germans.

'I'll get our friends together and we'll discuss what can be done,' Madame Passy said. 'Come and see me tomorrow afternoon.'

Len hurried back to Chemy. The Germans now knew for sure that a British escaped prisoner was operating with the French Resistance in the Gondecourt area. This meant that the Faucomprez family was in danger and he told Pierre and Fi-Fi that he would be moving on. But Fi-Fi had rationalised that Joe was merely some refugee scrounging free board and lodging by telling people that he was British, and Pierre agreed with her. When the parents took their daughters to Gondecourt next morning Len made plans for a quick escape in an emergency. He knew that the Germans nearly always raided a suspect house about two in the morning, hoping to take their victims asleep in bed. Also, they generally posted a dozen men at the back door before knocking on the front door.

His only way out was the roof. A door in the main bedroom led to an attic, full of the usual junk of packing cases and unused furniture and, in Pierre's case, of home-grown tobacco leaves hanging from the beams. In the roof of the attic was a pane of glass in a small metal frame, with a hooked stay to hold it open. The aperture was only twelve inches by eight but when he lifted the frame right out Len could just squeeze through by holding his arms straight above his head and narrowing his shoulders. He spent a full hour practising a rapid exit. Just along the roof was a large chimney stack, which might make a hiding place. Len left the frame lying on the roof and, satisfied that he could do no more in preparation, cycled to Gondecourt to see Madame Passy.

She had news. Her 'disposal specialists' had made arrangements for Joe to be invited to a banquet at the Cafe Delanghe, near the Grand Place. The invitation was innocent-sounding – some of the town's notables wanted a private opportunity to pass on a message of thanks to London. Furthermore, after the dinner Joe would be given a large sum of money to hand over to the Resistance. Four experienced men would be waiting and, at a given signal, Joe's career as a German agent would end. His grave, said Madame Passy, was even now being prepared in local marshland. The group was not to know that they had seriously underestimated Joe's intelligence and that he had plans of his own.

9

'THE TERRORIST LEONARD'

Two nights after Madame Passy had told Len of the plans to dispose of Joe, the Faucomprez family sat in the kitchen before going to bed. There was laughter and joking as the girls teased Len. Marcelle had a sense of humour and she liked to exercise it on the tall young Englishman who took everything so goodnaturedly.

When Tommy stalked to the back door and growled and barked, Len explored the back garden and looked into the street but he noticed nothing suspicious and they all went upstairs. Before going to bed Len checked the attic and found that Pierre had replaced the skylight cover to protect his tobacco from the cold; he removed it and placed it on the tiles again.

He always slept with the window open and a blanket hanging in place of a curtain so that he could hear everything that might be happening in the street. He also made good use of the dogs. Every household in every French village seemed to have a dog, all were kept in the yard, and all appeared to have hypersensitive hearing. When a stranger entered the village the first dog would bark and the alarm would pass from dog to dog until nobody could remain asleep. There was much barking that night and Fi-Fi called from her bedroom, 'I wonder why all the dogs are barking.'

'Probably Himmler is out there somewhere,' Len replied and they all laughed.

Despite the banter, he could not sleep until about two o'clock. And then he dreamed that battalions of British troops were marching through Chemy, their brightly polished boots clattering on the cobbles. In his dream Len cheered ecstatically and went searching for Pierre and Fi-Fi to tell them the good news. At that point he woke up suddenly – but part of the dream unaccountably continued. The boots were still marching.

Alarmed, with his pulse racing, Len jumped out of bed and peered around the blanket. Below him in the street stood about thirty fully armed, steel-helmeted German troops and they were shining powerful torches on the front of the house. Len ducked away as a beam settled on his window. As he struggled into his trousers rifle butts thumped on the front door and Pierre ran in to the room. 'What's the matter?' he asked, confused in his deep sleep.

'Germans!' Len said. 'And they've come for me! Keep them occupied while I get out through the roof.

'No, the back way!' Pierre urged him.

It was too late for the back way. As he spoke, at the bottom of the stairs appeared light from torches flashing through the windows and he heard the sounds of breaking glass as the troops battered down the back door. Len ran for the attic stairs as Pierre called out through the window, 'Who is that?'

'Open the door!' a German bellowed.

Because of his practice in projecting himself through the skylight Len was on the roof in five seconds and lying flat in the icy night as soldiers pounded into the attic. At any moment he expected a German head to appear six inches from his own through the aperture. Had the soldiers switched off their torches in the attic they might have noticed the lighter patch of night sky. They kicked around the furniture and cases and then clumped down the attic stairs. Len, freezing cold in only an old pair of trousers and a thin cotton vest, crawled along the sharply sloping roof, his bare feet giving him better grip than shoes on the tiles. Incredibly, the Germans did not shine their torches on the roof, though they hardly needed them. Had they just looked up carefully they must have seen the figure on the roof. Despite his predicament Len was more worried for the Faucomprez family than for himself for he feared that the troops might beat them up. Marcelle, who was just fourteen, must be terrified by the stampeding soldiers.

Two other roofs adjoined the Faucomprez house and Len crawled cautiously over them until he reached the end one. Looking down, he could just make out the roof of the next building, a farm. It was only one storey high, so Len lowered himself from the upper roof until he hung by his finger tips, but his searching toes could not find the lower roof. He had no grip to pull himself back so he simply let go and hoped for the best. He fell all of six inches – and into some mud that had collected there. Like an experienced cat burglar he slithered along the farm roof, jumped to an adjoining cowshed and was now in the Gondecourt road, only ten yards from the Germans who were just around the corner, watching the front of the house. Dropping to the cobbled road, he crossed quickly to a barbed wire fence, climbed over and was off across the open fields. As he crossed a beet patch a partridge rose between his running feet with a fearful screech and Len, startled out of his stride, fell heavily among the frost covered leaves where he lay panting, trying to calm his pounding heart. 'You idiot!' he told himself. 'You don't turn a hair when the German army tries to trap you and damn near faint over a bloody bird!'

As he picked himself up his thoughts were back at the house, wondering what had happened to his family – for the Faucomprezs were very much his family. Pierre had quickly hidden Len's clothes and gone downstairs with deliberate slowness and as he crossed the sitting room the soldiers who had entered through the smashed kitchen door pounded into him. The first man punched him hard in the chest and others hit him as they ran to open the front door. The men knew exactly where they were going – the result of Joe's reconnaissance.

Two rushed into Len's bedroom but Marcelle was now in the bed; Fi-Fi had realised that a warm, empty bed would arouse suspicions and sent Marcelle into Len's room. Six soldiers invaded the other room where Jervaise remained in the big double bed which she and Marcelle jointly used.

The soldiers dragged Fi-Fi downstairs to the kitchen where she recognised Joe, the 'British officer'. He snarled at her,

'Where is that English swine, Leonard?'

'I don't know what you are talking about,' she said calmly.

'We'll soon show you what we're talking about!' Joe said angrily.

Searching soldiers had let Tommy out of the coal shed and barking and snapping she tore into them, severely biting two before a heavy kick sent her flying back to the coal shed. Joe did not see the dog or he would certainly have recognised it as the animal which had terrorised him in Gondecourt.

Pierre was shoved into the sitting room where Joe and another officer loudly interrogated him, trying to bully him into inconsistencies. But Pierre Faucomprez was not a man to be rushed and he infuriated the officers with his considered replies. Fi-Fi, left alone in the kitchen for a few moments, realiséd with an appalled start that she was looking at Len's coat hanging behind the door. And in it, she knew, was his identity card in the name of Leonard Masseux. With complete sangfroid and deliberate courge she slipped the identity card from the pocket, pulled out the drawer of a wall cabinet and fastened the card underneath with a drawing pin.

Just as she replaced the drawer Joe entered the room. 'All right, Madame,' he said with the air of a man who had just solved a problem. 'Your husband has told us everything so you need not lie any more. Just tell us where we can find this terrorist Leonard and we will leave you in peace.'

Fi-Fi said patiently, 'I still don't know what you are talking about. I don't know any Leonard. The last English soldiers left here in 1940 and we have seen none since then.'

The angry Joe ordered another thorough search but an hour-long hunt produced nothing incriminating. As the Germans left at four a.m., Joe shouted at Pierre, 'We'll be back for you later!'

By then Len was safe. He had crossed the Gondecourt–Seclin railway line and made for the house of Adeline Cochet, who had first introduced Len to Pierre Faucomprez, her brother. As it was in a block of houses Len knocked softly and kept on knocking until he heard Adeline calling apprehensively through an upper window, 'Who's there?'

The noise of fast-moving vehicles came from the Seclin road and Len ran for cover as two cars full of Germans shot by. Again Len knocked and this time he was able to tell Adeline who he was – and again he had to dive for cover as more German cars tore past. By now Adeline was waiting behind the front door to let him slip inside. As he explained the emergency her eyes widened at his distressed condition.

'My God!' she said. 'Look at your feet!' Len had run two miles and his bare feet were bruised, cut and bloody. German cars were still roaring by and after he had eaten, treated his feet and acquired an old jacket and boots, Len made for a warm barn he knew of on the Seclin road. But worry about the Faucomprez family kept him restless and at 3.30 a.m. he set off to retrace his steps to Chemy. On the way he nearly met head-on the German company which had carried out the raid and dived flat among sugar beet leaves until the Germans had passed.

He approached the house in Chemy as a stalking soldier would, hugging the ground as he crawled. From the darkness he heard Fi-Fi calling softly, 'Joseph! Joseph!' and when Len answered she rushed to help him. Pierre was on the roof, also calling for 'Joseph'; they explained that they could hardly be heard calling 'Leonard' after denying the existence of anybody by that name. Jervaise and Marcelle were pale and trembling in the kitchen and Fi-Fi began to cry over the stove as shocked reaction to the German invasion set in. Len retrieved his clothing, which Pierre had hidden, and put on his overcoat before getting his bike. The family was against his leaving but Len could expose them no further to harassment and risk. He promised to return in a week and if it was safe by then Pierre was to hang a white cloth on a certain tree in Jerome Bulcourt's orchard.

Reluctantly, they agreed that it was safer for him to go and he embraced them and left abruptly to hide his own distress. These people were the first ever to take him in as a member of the family and he felt a depth of affection for them he had never before known. He cycled down the cold, dark and lonely road but soon became aware that somebody was following him on a bike. He speeded up and heard his pursuer's bike gaining speed. Riding flat out for a minute or so he veered off the road and flung himself flat with his bike beside him. As a dark figure appeared, peddling furiously, Len jumped up laughing; he had recognised Pierre. The older man gasped, 'I thought I would never catch you.'

'And I thought I had a bloody Boche after me,' Len said. 'What's up?'

Pierre handed him his identity card which Fi-Fi had belatedly remembered. 'Be careful, look after yourself,' he said and rode into the night back to Chemy. Len shook his head in real bewilderment, unable to understand why these simple country people ran such terrible risks for him. A patrolling Nazi soldier would shoot without question at anybody riding about at this hour of the night.

It was morning by the time Len reached Allennes-les-Marais and, still keyed up by the events of the night, he called at the Delcourt house where Alex Keiller was in hiding. Madame Delcourt was known as Madame Parapluie because her husband repaired umbrellas, but she was also known by less complimentary names as everybody knew of the affair she was having with Keiller. In fact, Keiller was also having an affair with her daughter and the family had become notorious. Madame Delcourt answered the door to Len's knock and said quickly that Keiller did not live there any more.

'That's a pity,' Len said. 'I'm Leonard, the Englishman from Gondecourt, and I have a message for him.'

A door burst open in the passage and Keiller stood there with bloodshot eyes. 'You bloody liar!' he shouted. 'Of course I'm here!' He abused her in vile French slang until Len interrupted him.

'I have come straight from Chemy to warn you that the Germans came for me last night. The agent who calls himself Joe was with them and he knows that you're here, so you are in as much danger as I was.' He watched Keiller's reaction closely, trying to discern if Keiller already knew Joe.

The Scot was silent, then gave Len a crafty look and said, 'I'm getting out of here.'

Len left at once and as he rode away he heard the man and woman still arguing at the tops of their voices.

In Annouellin, Madame Hochard, a widow who owned a butcher's shop, stopped him and took him home. This was a great risk for her because she had been released from prison not long before, after serving a sentence for harbouring a British escaper. Even now she was hiding a Scottish soldier escaper, whom Len had no difficulty in accepting as genuine. Mme Hochard offered Len sanctuary too, but he declined for the sake of her three children; one daughter was already in prison. The lady was resourceful and well connected and she sent one of her children for Joseph Wiplier, a large, stout and beaming man who worked in the coke works at Pont-à-Vendin. He was under the illusion that he spoke English fluently; as he told Len, 'Me speak very well, English.'

Known locally as 'Joseph dit Monsieur Louis' (Joseph the son of Monsieur Louis) Wiplier took Len to his home on the outskirts of Annouellin. Len noticed with approval that it was the last house of the town before the fields and trees and that there were no neighbours. He was thankful to be made welcome by Joseph's cheerful buxom wife, Lucienne, and to relax with a cup of tea.

The district was agog with news of the previous night's happenings in Chemy and Gondecourt. It became clear that afternoon that the local Resistance had suffered a disaster. The Germans had broken into Madame Passy's house and arrested her and her daughter Yvonne and they had taken Zelfa Ringot too. This news deeply depressed Len but he was exhausted and managed a few hours sleep before the Wiplier children came home from school. There were three – Henri, a big gawky lad of 13, Jo-Jo, 12 and pig-tailed Lucette, 9. After supper all three rested their chins on their hands, elbows on table, and stared at Len. He found their attention flattering but disconcerting. Lucienne and Joseph had already decided that he would sleep in their bedroom and that they would move in with the children.

But Len had been thinking deeply during the trauma of his near capture and he was determined never to sleep in a house where children were present. The Nazis made no allowances for children; in fact they were more likely to torture children than adults in the expectation that they would more rapidly break and give information. He asked the Wipliers for nothing more than a couple of old blankets and a groundsheet but the family was appalled that he proposed to sleep in the open with such skimpy covering and the children cried uncontrollably.

For the next three years whenever Len used Joseph's home in the daytime he would take to the fields at night, no matter the season or the weather. Sometimes the greatest risk came from the great shells fired by the anti-aircraft batteries at British planes; all this metal had to come to ground and sometimes it seemed to Len that he was right underneath the bursting flak. It thudded into the ground all around him. At dawn, with the risk of a Gestapo night house raid over, he returned to the house. And always the Wiplier children waited for him, refusing to go to school until they knew he was safe and under shelter. Sometimes he had had little sleep and the cold had penetrated to his bones but he managed to cover up his discomfort and weariness.

Now that he had found a safe house and learnt the dreadful news about Madame Passy, her daughter Yvonne and Zelfa Ringot, Len checked on Stan and Jack. They had returned to the Dubureaux house for good, he was told. Len gave them up as hopeless; he had done all he could to save them.

For the Germans, Lille was one of the most important cities in France. Many of the nation's largest factories were situated there and the junction and sidings were a key part of the railway system. There were many 'natural' targets for saboteurs and the Resistance, as well as for the RAF Only a few days after Len had been driven out of Gondecourt and Chemy the RAF raided the Lille railway yards, which were protected by scores of anti-aircraft guns. During the tremendous barrage, a Spitfire escorting the bombers was shot down and the pilot parachuted towards Allennes-les-Marais. Hundreds of people from many villages nearby converged on the spot, Len among them. He was among the first to reach the pilot, to find that he had been badly burnt about the face. A trained nurse was already painting his wounds with a yellow liquid.

Kneeling beside the pilot, Len said, 'How about escaping before the Germans get here? I can get you away.'

He was startled when the man answered in what he thought was German. 'He's Polish,' the nurse said, 'and he's so badly burned he must have hospital treatment. You can't help him.'

Len was immensely disappointed; he had hoped to send the pilot back to England. By now more than a thousand people had gathered and a murmur arose as four German soldiers on horseback came galloping over the fields. 'You really can do nothing for him,' the nurse told Len and gave him a gentle push away as if she knew his own danger. It was time for him to leave and he made his way disconsolately to Annoeullin.

A week later his fear for Pierre and his family drove him to Chemy and he was delighted to see a white handkerchief fluttering as a signal from the tree in the orchard. He was greeted by cries of delight and Marcelle particularly hugged and kissed him. 'You see!' Pierre said triumphantly. 'They have no proof that you were here and they have probably forgotten all about the whole thing. We are all safe.'

Len wished he could believe this but he understood more about the Nazis than Pierre did. It was obvious that the Nazis had not given up the hunt because they had put up WANTED posters; one was on the wall opposite the Faucomprez house. It referred to him as 'the terrorist Leonard' and most alarmingly his photograph appeared on the poster. Len's apprehension was still so acute that he stayed no longer than an hour before returning to the Wiplier house; collecting his blankets, he disappeared into the fields.

Next morning visitors brought the news that the Germans were very active. Field police were checking all papers and identity cards in trains and buses and Gestapo agents were present in force to make the same check with cyclists. Len was consumed with worry and later that day his worst fears came true. Joseph came home to say that the Germans had returned to Chemy and had surrounded the house, as before. After searching it, they individually interrogated all four people and had arrested Pierre and Jervaise, who were taken to Loos prison. The leader told the shocked Fi-Fi, 'You have a week to tell us where to find this Englander Leonard.' And he mockingly saluted in farewell.

Len, too, was shocked. 'I am going to give myself up,' he told Joeph. 'I can't allow the Nazis to shoot the whole family.'

The normally placid Joseph was furiously angry and in his exasperation he characteristically tugged at his central tuft of hair. 'Are you mad! Have you completely lost your head? If you give yourslf up then they will certainly be shot.' He snapped his fingers. 'Just like that. And then the incident will be closed. As long as the Nazis do not catch you the Faucomprezs are safe.'

He was so insistent, as was his wife, that Len yielded to their judgment. But he was determined to see Fi-Fi, though he kept this from Joseph; he did not need to be told that this action was dangerous and could be fatal. He kept away from Pierre's house and entering the village across the fields after dark he went to the house of Auntie Marianne, near the church. The lady herself opened the door to his knock, exclaimed in horror, 'Good God, it's Leonard!' and went to slam the door in his face. Len jammed his foot in it. 'I want to see Fi-Fi,' he said, 'and I'm not leaving until I do.'

'Fi-Fi is not here,' Marianne snapped.

'Then go and fetch her.'

'Who is it?' somebody called from inside and Julienne Delannoy appeared. Julienne was a niece of Auntie Denise from Loos-les-Lille and a level-headed girl. 'All right,' she said when told of Len's demand. 'He can see her outside. I'll call her.'

She returned a few minutes later with Fi-Fi and Marcelle, both weeping and in near collapse with shock, fear and exhaustion. Len hugged both of them and, blaming himself for their plight, was near tears himself. Julienne, afraid that the little group would draw unwelcome attention, shepherded them to the privacy of the old village school.

Len said determinedly, 'If the Germans will set Pierre and Jervaise free I will give myself up.'

Marcelle was horrified. 'If you do that the Germans will shoot you!'

Len was equally sure this would happen but he merely said, 'It's your mother's decision.'

'No,' Fi-Fi said emphatically. 'It would be better if we wait awhile. There's just a chance that the Germans will release Papa and Jervaise.'

Len agreed. 'All right,' he said, 'let us wait. But no matter what happens I will keep in touch with you.'

He broke off the meeting. With the Germans so active even minutes could be dangerous. After embracing the women again and thanking Julienne he left for Annouellin, reflecting that matters could hardly be worse. 'Those bastards are after you Len,' he told himself as he cycled through the night, 'and they won't let up.'

A week later, at six in the morning and fresh from his sleeping place in the fields, he waited by the side of the track leading to Gondecourt station. He knew that Marcelle cycled this way on her way to work in the cotton factory in Seclin. Daylight would not appear for some time yet and he knew he was safe enough, though when he stepped out and stopped Marcelle he cursed himself for clumsiness. Already the tense girl was trembling with fright and she started to cry. Her anxiety was for him. 'You must go, Len,' she sobbed, as they embraced and kissed. 'The Germans have men everywhere looking for you. They came around again last night and this morning I saw two men hanging around Auntie Denise's house.'

'I'm safe, really, I am,' Len said. 'But how's Fi-Fi?'

'She's very worried about Papa and Jervaise.'

'I'll come around one evening, after dark,' Len suggested.

'No, no! It's too dangerous. Keep away for a while.'

Miserable and anxious Len kissed her again and let her go to work. That night the Germans were back in Chemy, terrorising Fi-Fi and Marcelle. After more fruitless interrogation the leader said, 'Very well, Madame, we will take your daughter to join her father and sister in prison. We will leave you on your own for a few weeks to give you time to think. You can worry about what might happen to your family. When you tell us where to find Leonard they will all be freed.'

Marcelle, frantic with fear and grief, clung to her mother. The German soldiers pulled them apart and carried Marcelle, kicking and shouting, to a car. Fi-Fi, distraught and tearful, was afraid to stay alone in the house and went to her brother Simeon, who lived just around the corner. He turned her away. 'I'm having nothing to do with you,' he said through a partly-opened door. 'Do you think I want to finish up in gaol?'

His wife, Denise, shocked by his attitude, tried to get him to change his mind. When he still refused Denise left home and spent the night with Fi-Fi.

Anxious for news, Fi-Fi visited her elder sister Jermaine, who lived in the Lille suburb of Loos. Her husband was a postman and his round included the prison, where he had contacts, but all he could learn was that the three Faucomprez prisoners were kept in the part of the prison taken over by the Gestapo.

Fi-Fi induced her brother-in-law to take her to the prison but they were refused entry and on the way back they were followed by two Gestapo thugs who forced their way into Jermaine's house and searched it. On the kitchen table they found a letter from friends, with whom Jermaine's son was staying. As they read it, they pounced on the sentence, 'The big son is doing well but could do with a few kilos of haricot beans as he is always hungry.' The senior Gestapo man laughed. 'So the big son would like haricot beans! This big son could just be our old friend Leonard and we will see he gets some haricot beans!'

By now the hunt for Leonard had become an obsession with the Gestapo and field police. Sooner or later they picked up all escapers and evaders – other than some airmen passed quickly through the district along a life-line – but Leonard had been at large longer than anybody.

Returning to Chemy, Fi-Fi was still reluctant to stay in her empty house and called to ask Denise to spend the night with her. This time her brother refused to let her even speak to Denise. 'Just go away,' he said roughly. 'I have forbidden Denise to go to your house.'

'Let me in for a little while, please,' Fi-Fi pleaded.

'Go!' her brother said, and closed the door.

As her brother, her natural protector, would not help her Fi-Fi went to her sister Marianne, but her door was locked and bolted and she refused to open it. She had the same blunt and harsh rejection from two other sisters, Simone and Fideline, who lived in the village. As Fi-Fi sobbed against a wall near Marianne's house a door opened across the road and a friendly and anxious voice said, 'What's going on? What's the trouble? Fi-Fi, is that you?'

This was Madame Marthe Roussel, whose husband was a prisoner of war in Germany. She hurried across the road, friendly and consoling, 'Come into my warm kitchen and you can tell me about it over a cup of coffee.' Overwhelmed by her kindness after her own family's rejection, Fi-Fi broke down completely. Mme Roussel kept Fi-Fi in her house, saying grimly, 'Tomorrow I will have a word with Marianne! We are all French, are we not, and we will act as French people. You will stay here with me as long as necessary.'

As they promised, the Germans gave Fi-Fi 'time to think' – three weeks, in fact. A breathless villager arrived late one evening to say that a carload of Boche had turned up and were looking for Fi-Fi at her house. 'Bring the Boche here,' Madame Roussel said. 'Tell them Madame Foucomprez will be waiting for them.'

While she waited, the trembling Fi-Fi gathered her few possessions and soon there came the characteristic thumping of rifle butts on the door. 'Courage, Fi-Fi,' Mme Roussel said, and with disdain written in every gesture admitted the strutting German officers. Though shaking, Fi-Fi faced them.

'Madame Faucomprez?' one asked.

'Yes,' Fi-Fi said.

'Why are you hiding here, instead of being in your own home?'

Marthe Roussel answered for her. 'Madame Faucomprez is not hiding. She has no need to hide. She has been unwell, too unwell to stay on her own. I have been looking after her.'

The officer shrugged. 'Come with us,' he ordered Fi-Fi. She gave Marthe a despairing look and went with them. Driven to Loos prison she was put into solitary confinement in a pitch black cell. Terrified, and with mice rustling across her feet all night, she had no sleep. In the morning silent German guards came for her and led her through long corridors to an office where two other German officers sat at a desk.

In excellent French, one said, 'We are going to bring your husband in here but we want to warn you that he is in a very bad way, though no fault of ours.'

Fi-Fi nearly collapsed, but she said fiercely, 'What have you done to him?' In recent weeks she had learned much about Nazi methods of interrogation and torture.

'Nothing has happened to him!' the officer snapped. 'He has had a bad attack of boils on his face and neck. This morning a surgeon has had to lance the boils so his face and neck are covered with bandages.' As he finished speaking Pierre came in between guards, only his eyes and nose visible through bandages – paper bandages since cloth was unobtainable. He and Fi-Fi were not allowed to embrace and the officer instructed Pierre to tell Fi-Fi that he had suffered no ill-treatment at German hands. This was true enough in a strictly physical sense and Pierre confirmed it. The officer went on, 'You are being held in prison accused of harbouring enemy agents. This is punishable with the death penalty. The tribunal will sit shortly.'

Pierre said in a muffled but calm voice, 'Why are our children being held?'

'They are accused of not denouncing their parents' illegal activities to the occupation authorities.' The officer's tone made this 'crime' sound heinous.

Two weeks later, at the end of 1941, the 'Gondecourt gang' were brought before a tribunal. There were Pierre and Sophie (Fi-Fi) Faucomprez, Jervaise and Marcelle, and Zelfa Ringot, though she was not tried in company with the Faucomprez family.

The prosecutor was direct when he questioned Pierre. 'Why did you hide the escaped prisoner Leonard in your house?'

Pierre had long since decided that denial was not only

pointless but antagonistic to the Germans. 'I did not hide him because he was a British soldier,' he said, 'but because I am a father and I found this young man wandering around starving, and sleeping in open fields.' It was the best possible story.

The officer smiled thinly. 'And what if this young man had been German? Would your fatherly instincts have prompted you to shelter him?'

'Yes, of course!' Pierre said. 'Without hesitation I would.'

This reply was so apparently sincere that it impressed the officer, who cut short the hearing. The prisoners were led out while the tribunal conferred. Brought back to the courtroom the fmaily listened to the senior officer who delivered the sentences.

When he and the other Germans pronounced the Faucomprez name they emphasised the last syllable with a harsh prez, unlike the normal unstressed French prey.

'Faucomprez, Pierre, you are sentenced to four years hard labour in a fortress prison in Germany.'

'Faucomprez, Sophie, you are sentenced to one year in the civilian prison of Loos.'

'Faucomprez, Jervaise, you are sentenced to six months in the civilian prison of Loos.'

'Faucomprez, Marcelle, you are sentenced to six months in the civilian prison of Loos.' Marcelle had the dubious distinction of being the youngest prisoner of the Nazis in that gaol.

Pierre was at once separated from his family and had time for only a brief wave of the hand. For the three women the trial and conviction ended weeks of privation in the Gestapo cells. Now they would be transferred to the civilian section, under French female warders, most of whom were reasonable and humane.

Zelfa Ringot was also sentenced to a year in the same prison. Madame Passy was not formally tried. As a 'very dangerous' person she was simply sentenced to death by faceless, anonymous 'Authority'. Before she was parted from the other women she contrived one day to meet Marcelle when the women were taken under guard to the showers. She and the girl shared the same shower and Madame Passy indicated to Marcelle to get onto her knees behind her so that the warder would not notice that they were speaking together.

'I haven't much time,' she said, 'so listen carefully. Marcelle, I know that you are a patriotic young girl and that I can trust you. When you are freed go to Madame Delanghe in Gondecourt and tell her that I was betrayed by Henriette Verbeke, whose lover is a Gestapo agent. She will know what to do. Promise me this.'

This was a heavy responsibility for a young girl. Marcelle gave her promise and she kept it.

Put on one of the many trains taking condemned people to Germany, Madame Passy finished up in Ravensbruck, the infamous concentration camp for women. She perished in the gas chambers shortly after her arrival. She did not go unavenged.*

Len, thoroughly depressed by the arrest of Fi-Fi, wisely listened to the advice of his friends not to surrender himself. All of them knew of similar cases in which a hunted man had given himself up to save hostages only to have the Germans then kill them. But it was a hard decision. Every instinct in him cried out to surrender and save 'his' family. He felt bereft.

---

* See *And Afterwards*.

10

COLLECTING SAFE HOUSES

The Nazis were intent on catching all escaped British soldiers because they were a constant reminder to the French people that Britain was still fighting against the German oppressors. Also, these soldiers who joined the Resistance movement became links between various Resistance groups and London. Many *réseaus* or cells functioned around a British officer; often they were inspired by him and trained, financed and armed by him. The Nazi occupation authorities had an almost neurotic compulsion to eliminate all British influence from occupied France. And when they knew of the existence of an Englishman, as they knew about Len Arlington, and could not trap him they became as angry with themselves as they did with those people who protected him.

Most British evaders and escapers — as distinct from those specially trained officers who were parachuted into France to organise resistance — were caught not so much as a result of German cleverness but as the consequence of their own foolishness and carelessness. This did not apply to Len Arlington. He was prepared to endure great hardship to elude his pursuers, even to the extent of sleeping in the open in mid-winter. Perhaps even more important, he could exist alone without losing his nerve or succumbing to the natural temptation to find friendly company. His inner resources were as much a protection as his resourcefulness. In contrast, his friends Jack and Stan, in Berclau-Haisnes, were living as if the war was a game, a risky game perhaps, but one which kept its distance from them. Theirs was a comfortable enough life, especially in the Dubureaux home, and they became more relaxed – and then lax and careless. The two men had noticed that Len was ever alert and looking around for possible trouble, and they had seen from his example that it was possible to be a loner yet not become depressed but his type of rough and ready life on the run did not appeal to them. Len could not understand their attitude, because there was no shortage of reports about Gestapo brutality to people caught helping the hated British enemy. But he had some advantages over Jack and Stan; most importantly he had come to know people in this area before the shooting war had started in May 1940 while Jack and Stan had come from St Valery, many miles away. Also, they lacked his Cockney self-assurance and his gregarious ability to make friends quickly.

On January 27 1942 Jack and Stan were trapped by Bruno and other Gestapo agents, as well as forty German soldiers, in the Dubureaux home. Jack tried to escape over the roofs, as Len had done, but the Germans were not to be eluded this time and he had the choice of climbing down or being shot down. Both men were sent to Bethune prison and were transferred on February 14 to Gestapo HQ in Arras. They were taken to the cellars and put separately in solitary confinement cells. Kept awake by night they were tortured and harassed during the day. Bruno and the gaolers made a habit of kicking the shins of their captives while interrogating them.

M. and Mme Dubureaux and their daughter Huguette were arrested at the same time as the soldiers. The Resistance intelligence system reported that Jack and Stan had somehow gained the idea – probably from the Germans – that M. Andrieux was dying of some malignant disease. They decided to put all the blame on him, as he would soon be dead anyway, and in the belief that the Germans would be satisfied to lay their hands on the 'ringleader' and would leave the others alone. Andrieux could not stand up to torture and gave the Gestapo a name or two; then one by one frightened victims denounced one another. The Gestapo drafted in more investigators, the sabotage at Finalens chemical works was discovered and Victor Dejong, the Finalens company director, and the cafe owner, Leignel, joined the list of those arrested. In all, the Germans took fifty people.

Without difficulty, considering the appalling lack of security among the members of the Berclau-Haisnes group, the Gestapo discovered Len's connections with them and the order went out to 'get the Englishman Leonard at all costs'. In cash terms, 'all costs' meant 100,000 francs – the reward figure shown on the WANTED posters.

Really alarmed when this news reached him, Len hardly dared move from Joseph Wiplier's house during the day. This house was the last in Annouellin on a small track leading in the general direction of Provin. The Germans heard that he was hidden in the last house on the Provin road itself and it was no accident that they formed this impression – Len had accidentally-on-purpose let the information slip during a conversation with a man he suspected of being a Gestapo informer. In a two a.m. raid, fifty troops surrounded the house. One group leapt over a low wall and two men fell flat on their faces in pig dung while two others were up to their knees in the muck, as the farmer and his wife witnessed from their window. The Gestapo chief quickly realised that the pair were innocent and withdrew his men; throughout the district the story spread that the German pigs had fallen into their own stinking filth. It was good for morale. The Germans continued to swoop on private houses in their search for Len, who was mostly at this time in Lucienne Wiplier's kitchen.

It was here that he heard terrible news. The Germans had posted a proclamation that for 'terrorist activities' Dejong, Leignel, Dubureaux and Andrieux had been shot by firing squad. Executions had been expected but still they came as a shock. That night was bitterly cold and snow was falling heavily as Len gathered his bedding to leave for the fields.

Joseph, appalled, said, 'You're not going outside to sleep in this?'

'Joseph,' Len said, 'You have seen what happened in Berclau. I will not run the risk of being caught in your house, with all that this would mean for you and your family.'

'My God, you're stubborn.' Joseph said. 'All right, but let's go and see a friend of mine. I know that he is willing to put you up for the night if you leave first thing in the morning.'

The friend was René Saublin, who lived at 98 Route de Don. A small, very plump man, Saublin was wearing a white coat and a black beret when he opened the door and Len noticed that every one of his teeth had been plated with gold – Saublin was a dental mechanic. Len thought that when Saublin smiled it was like looking into a bullion vault. A Belgian, though resident in France, he had sustained two broken legs and multiple injuries in 1939 when his car was in collision with a British army truck. He, his wife and his eighty-year-old mother welcomed Len at once and gave no sign that they were worried by the danger he posed for them. Saublin and Len talked about the war late into the night and Saublin had a good idea. 'You should find at least a dozen safe houses, Leonard,' he said, 'people who would be willing to put you up for a night or two. Try to keep all these people ignorant of the existence of the others. If one were to be caught there would not be the disaster that happened at Berclau-Haisnes. You just keep on the move from one house to another.'

Len was no procrastinator and put the idea into effect next day. Cycling through Fournes, he stopped at Le Moulin Rouge cafe, ordered a glass of beer from an elderly woman and leaned against the bar. She tapped her nose knowingly. 'M'seiur,' she said, 'you are English, aren't you?'

Len thought, '*God, will I never look like a Frenchman to Frenchmen!*' He said casually, 'What makes you say that?'

The woman laughed. 'I was with British troops all through the last war. I can tell a Tommy anywhere.'

'You certainly spotted this one,' Len said ruefully, 'and I'm glad you did. I'm looking for somebody who can give me shelter now and then.'

This chance meeting opened doors. The woman sent Len to her brother, Desiré Trenelle, in Rue d'Estaires, La Bassée, six miles away, and he too was willing to help. That night Trenelle introduced Len to a farmer, Achille Bliez, who also instantly identified Len as English. Next day he met Achille's sister, Lea Desmarais, whose first words were, 'But he's English!'

He went home with Lea and met her nineteen-year-old son, Paul, a strapping young man who was delighted to be protecting a British soldier. Lea proposed giving Len a key to her house, but Len was too shrewd to accept it. 'If I ever get caught,' he said, 'the Germans will beat hell out of me to find out to whose house that key belongs – and they might break me. Their tortures are terrible and I wouldn't like to promise that I could stay silent.' The Gestapo torturers were notorious for pulling out their victims' fingernails and toenails one by one, and for the way they used electricity on sensitive parts of the body. In Lille one of the worst sadists used to clamp a victim's arm in a vice and then sew his fingers one to the other with needle and thread. Len had been thinking of ways of killing himself before he could betray his friends under torture.

Paul had a solution to the problem of the key. A boy after Len's own heart, he gave him a lockpick, a thick piece of copper wire about three inches long and bent over half an inch, and taught him how to use it. Such an implement identified no particular house.

That evening Len unburdened himself to Lea about his worry over the Faucomprez family. Lea, a dominant woman accustomed to getting her own way, said, 'Suppose I go to the prison and see them?'

'It wouldn't be possible,' Len said.

'I can try,' Lea said and changed the subject. Next morning she cycled to Lille, taking two packets of Gitanes cigarettes for Pierre, should she see him. Len waited anxiously all day and knew at once from Lea's delighted eyes when she returned that evening, that she had been successful.

'This was the very day allowed for visits and I arrived at the right hour. I saw Pierre and spoke with him for over an hour.' Her tone was triumphant.

Len was astonished. 'But only close relatives are allowed to see prisoners.'

'Of course,' Lea said airily, 'and I am the latest member of

Pierre's family. I am his sister. But we can improve on all this. Why don't you come to the prison to visit Pierre. I'll tell the Germans you are my son.'

Len was greatly tempted but left the decision to Pierre, when Lea would visit him again. Not surprisingly, Pierre sent word that the risk was too great.

Meanwhile, Joseph Wiplier had found two more safe houses. One was at Provin, the home of Felicien Lemaire; his house could be easily reached by following a track across the fields from Joseph's home. The second hideout was in the Sion Cafe, near the Grand Place of Annouellin, owned by Antoine Sion and his wife, Amelie, both middle-aged and worldly wise. Joseph took Len through the cafe into the back kitchen and Len, always anxious for escape routes, gestured to the door. 'What's out there?'

Sion opened the door to reveal a huge hall. 'It used to be a place for banquets,' he said. 'Now a whole German infantry battalion lives there.'

'Blimey!' Len said. 'A whole blooming battalion!'

'And most of them pass through the cafe coming and going to the hall,' Sion said with a smile. 'But don't worry. Do you suppose a Gestapo man would expect you to be staying here?'

'Not one in his right mind,' Len said. He was not sure he was in his right mind in accepting the Sion Cafe as a safe house but the older man's confidence was catching. Over the next two and a half years Len found that Amelie Sion was one of the most reliable of all his helpers. She asked no questions but understood his problems at once and acted incisively.

On his own volition, Len found more safe houses. One was on a lonely farm at Illies, near Laventie, owned by M. Lestoquoi, and another at Lens, owned by a coal miner, M. Puchois. Three others followed, at Cuinchy-les-Mines near Bethune, Salome near La Bassée and at Hanay.

Meanwhile, in Gondecourt the sisters Marie-Sophie and Florentine were facing a terrible emergency. A local man, Guelton, over six feet tall and powerful, had been engaged in black market business with a German sergeant who was in the medical corps. The sergeant made the mistake of having an affair with Guelton's girl friend. Guelton, a violent and possessive man, lured the German to a lonely spot on the pretext of discussing black market transactions, and then buried his sheath knife to the hilt in the man's back. He dumped the German's bike in a canal and dug a shallow grave and buried the body, having already rammed the man's head into a rusty old bucket. Next morning Paul, Marie-Sophie's son, was on a poaching expedition when his dog, Izzy, raised his hind leg over something sticking from the ground. It was a human hand. Paul ran for his mother and she and Florentine, armed with shovels, uncovered the body. When they saw the field-grey uniform on the corpse they knew at once that this was a crisis and they sought the help of Madame Passy's gamekeeper, Leon. Alarmed, he said, 'If the Germans discover that corpse on private land half the people at Gondecourt will be killed in reprisals. We must dig it up and rebury it deeply in the woods.'

Florentine now showed the same cool nerve that her sister had demonstrated when rescuing Young and Wilson from among the German troops in the cafe. Taking charge of the operation she said, 'Very well, we'll do it tonight – and not a word to anybody else.'

Leon would not even touch the corpse and wanted nothing to do with moving it but he agreed to dig a grave in the woods. The women unearthed the sergeant and as they had no transport Florentine, a slight but strong and determined woman, carried the corpse on her back, with its heels tracking on the ground behind her. It was four in the morning before they had set the turf over the new grave and smoothed the soil over the old one.

The Germans raised the alarm that morning and the Gestapo was quickly on the scene. Before long they knew that the sergeant had been seen with Guelton who, tough though he was, broke down under torture and confessed. He led the Germans to the spot where he had buried his victim. No trace remained, for Florentine and Marie-Sophie had done a thorough job. Even tracker dogs failed to pick up any scent and the empty grave was not found. Since the Germans regarded death by firing squad as a military honour, Guelton was decapitated. By taking the body from private land and concealing it the two women had saved the town from being incriminated in the murder.

The Germans now had 500 troops searching for Len Arlington and early in December 1941 they had heard that he was hiding on a farm in the La Bassée area. They swamped the district with at least a thousand soldiers, raiding every farm within a radius of five miles. Included was Achille Bliez's farm but nothing incriminating was found. At the time Len was in Annouellin. The frustrated Gestapo liberated Marcelle and Jervaise Faucomprez on the pretext that this was an example of their Christmas goodwill, but they were a bait. The girls returned to Chemy and the Germans watched the village closely, convinced that Len would be drawn to it because of his concern for the girls; they might also have realised that by now Len had more than a brotherly interest in Marcelle. Len knew that the house would be watched and kept well away; after two weeks the Germans gave up and returned the girls to Loos prison. It was at this time that Len slipped through the clutches of 'Captain Jack Evans', who had his revenge with the arrest of Lucien and Ernest Lemaire.

Early in 1942 a senior Nazi official, on a general tour of northern France, visited the Gestapo section of Loos prison and the inmates were ordered to stand by the door of their cells for his inspection. Followed by a retinue of at least twenty, the black-uniformed VIP Nazi merely glanced at most of the women. His glistening jackboots came to a stop when he drew level with Marcelle.

'Why are you here?' he demanded.

'Because my parents gave shelter to an escaped British prisoner of war, sir,' she said.

'And how old are you?' His tone was ominous and Marcelle was worried.

'Fourteen years and six months, sir.'

'*What age?*' the officer said incredulously.

'Fourteen years and six months.'

The man turned and shouted at his subordinates 'Since when has the German nation declared war on children! I want any infants out of this prison immediately!'

His word was law and within two hours Marcelle – and because of her Jervaise also – were waiting in Lille for the bus to Gondecourt. It was already overcrowded, with not even standing room, but the driver, Maurice Doornaert, knew about the Faucomprez girls. He stood up and shouted into the bus, 'These two patriots have just come out of a Nazi prison and I'm not leaving them behind. A couple of you men, get out and climb onto the luggage rack.' The passengers cheered, three young men clambered onto the roof and Jervaise and Marcelle travelled the ten miles home in style and free of charge.

Len's Intelligence sources were good and he heard that very night, in Sion Cafe, Annoeullin, that the Faucomprez girls had been freed. The following night he cycled to Chemy, hid his bike and crept to the back window of their house. He heard Jervaise and Marcelle but as there was also a third and strange voice he thought it best not to show himself and was stealing away when he sensed that he was being watched and then followed. He drew his razor-sharp sheath knife. His follower was Auntie Denise, who never knew how close she came to be stabbed. Len put the weapon away hurriedly when he recognised her. He had a long talk with her, learning that Pierre had finally been taken to Germany, that Fi-Fi was sick with worry about her daughters and that Marianne, perhaps to make up for her earlier cruelty to Fi-Fi, was taking the girls into her home.

Much of her news was heartening and, best of all, she gave Len a photograph of Marcelle taken on her release from prison. He was delighted to have it though he knew that if the Gestapo found it on him it was hopelessly incriminating; there would be no pretending that he was not the Leonard for whom they were searching.

As Len cycled away from Auntie Denise and through the darkened village of Chemy at eleven p.m. he passed a shadowy figure standing on the pavement and peering to see who was

rash enough to be out so late after curfew. This man called
'M'sieur! Vos lumière!' ('Your light!')

No lights were allowed on any vehicle or bike after dark but
Len was using a handheld torch with a beam of 100 yards. He
thought the man was a busybody and snarled some foul advice
to him in crude patois. More politely put, it meant 'Mind your
own business!' Had Len recognised M. Delfosse, the mayor, he
would have realised that he was being given a friendly warning.
He did not hear Delfosse call out to Marcelle, leaning from an
upper window, 'He's very rude, isn't he?'

Feeling relaxed because he knew the girls were safe, Len
broke into a whistle as he passed the church – and his torch
picked out about twenty Nazi soldiers standing in a group
outside the old village prison near the school. 'Gorblimey Len,'
he said, 'now you've torn it!' If he turned back he damned
himself, so he went on at greater speed, now acutely aware of
the photograph in his pocket and of the sheath knife, which the
Germans classed as a 'terrorist' weapon. When he had drawn
nearly level with the Germans it seemed as if they would let
him pass. Then a young officer stepped into the road, one hand
raised, the other holding a revolver.

'Halte, m'sieur!' he called.

Len gave him the same rude advice that he had given the
mayor and standing on his pedals he raced past the enemy
patrol. The amazed officer screamed, 'Halte, halte, halte!' and
emptied his revolver after the fugitive. Len heard him yelling at
his men to fire and at a distance of about 200 yards a volley of
rifle bullets cracked past him. Ahead of him a car engine roared
into life and twin beams of light flashed in his direction.
Instantly, he turned off the road, jumped off the bike and ran
with it into a field with piles of just gathered sugar beet. The
car sped back the way Len had come. He was safe for the
moment but soon road blocks would be in position and he had
to reach any safe house at Annouellin. Local knowledge paid
off. He ran the 500 yards to the railway line, leapt onto his bike
and rode like a champion sprinter along the cinder track beside
the line, which took him into Annoeullin without his having to

use a single road. But it was a race against time for beams of light showed that the car was also heading for the town, more or less parallel to the railway. Len reached Joseph Wiplier's house perhaps a minute before the Germans screeched into the town. It was one of his narrowest escapes.

Joseph found out next day that the soldiers' presence in Chemy had no connection with the Faucomprez girls; they had arrived to investigate a bonfire which might have been a signal for a parachute drop to the Resistance.

A day or so later, after a night spent elsewhere, Len reached the Wiplier home early in the morning to find the three children in noisy argument. As he sat in the high wicker chair, his recognised place in the house, he said to Lucienne, 'What's the fuss about?'

Nine-year-old Lucette gave her mother no chance to reply. Running into the room, she presented Len with three small bars of chocolate and said, 'This is your chocolate ration.'

'What do you mean?' Len asked. 'I have no chocolate ration.'

'Yes you have, Leonard, and this is it,' the child said and ran out to continue the argument with her brothers.

Lucienne explained. 'Yesterday the children received their official chocolate ration, just four small bars each. They have had a conference and the three piles of four bars have been changed into four piles of three bars. One is your ration. That's their decision.'

'But the argument I heard?'

'They have been trying to do each other out of bars,' Lucienne said. 'And Jo-Jo managed to get one of Lucette's – that was the row you heard. Your share has been on the mantelpiece and was sacred.'

Len, the boy who had never had a family and to whom the world of gift-giving was alien, was overwhelmed. Unable to say much for the very real British fear of being emotional, he thanked the children individually by shaking their hands and put the chocolate in his pocket. He knew that they would be deeply offended if he gave it back to them.

The simplicity of most of his friends never ceased to surprise him and he had an example that morning, as he watched Lucienne preparing a large pile of laundry which she did for the wife of a local farmer. The money she earned helped with the family income, she said. This morning she went out to buy washing soap on the black market and when she returned Len asked, 'How much did you pay for the soap?'

Lucienne grimaced. 'One hundred and twenty francs for the kilo.'

'And how many washes can you do with a kilo?'

'About four.'

'And how much do you charge for a day's laundry?'

'Twenty-five francs,' Lucienne said, almost apologetically.

Len said gently, 'Lucienne, you are paying the farmer's wife for the privilege of doing her laundry. Don't you realise that?'

Lucienne stood for nearly a minute with her mouth open in disbelief. Then abruptly she picked up the washing and marched around to the farm. Throwing the basket at the feet of the amazed woman, she said angrily, 'For that price you can do your own dirty laundry!'

She and Len never spoke of the matter again. Her ignorance was explicable. Orphaned when young, she had spent her childhood near the front lines of World War I where there had been no opportunity for schooling. She had worked from early childhood in the fields and could neither read nor write and profits meant nothing to her. All she had, really, this fresh-faced green-eyed woman, was a big heart.

II

'HERR GENERALE LEE-ON-AR'' LIVES DANGEROUSLY

While some French men and women were actively patriotic and resisted the Germans in one way or another a good many others were passive, and though they did not help the Germans they wanted no part in Resistance work. Some helped the Resistance only as a form of insurance for the day of reckoning when the occupation would end. One such man was the tobacco farmer Lestoquoi, who had become wealthy through black market deals. Len disliked the man but because his farm was isolated he sometimes stayed there. One night he counted fifty smugglers who assembled at the farm to collect tobacco. Len asked the wealthy Lestoquoi for some tobacco for 'a patriot', Pierre Faucomprez, suffering in a Nazi prison, and was shocked when Lestoquoi charged him 100 francs for about a pound of poor quality leaf.

After this blatant profiteering Len had no qualms about stealing from Lestoquoi and as he slept in one of the curing rooms his opportunities for theft were frequent. He stole good quality tobacco leaves, which Joseph Wiplier sold in the mines; some of the money went to Lucienne for housekeeping. Len put straps around his trouser legs to hold the tobacco and on one occasion he had so much stuffed down the legs his trousers looked like plus fours.

Astonishingly, throughout his years of evading the Germans, Len was never short of money; seldom did he have less than 200 francs in his pocket. People he hardly knew would hand him money just as a means of doing something, anything, against the Germans. Unable to fight, they gained some satisfaction from being able to help a British soldier. One man, who had been bragging about his friendship with 'Leonard, the British Intelligence officer', refused to let him spend a night in his house but he eased his guilty conscience with the gift of 1,000 francs. Len buried this money in a flower pot in the Wiplier's garden, as an emergency hoard.

Dr Dupas, a professor of medicine in Lille, and his family were genuinely generous. Throughout the war Mme Dupas sent parcels of food to the Faucomprez family, and often there was money or something special marked 'for the Englishman'. Fortunately, none of these parcels was ever intercepted and searched by the Gestapo.

Len had other money from the sale of the stolen Lestoquoi tobacco and at no time did he have to ask for cash. His friends would not even ask if he needed it; they pushed it into his palm and closed his fingers around it, or thrust it deep into his pocket and walked away quickly. This generosity never ceased to amaze him. Possession of money enabled him to pay for his keep in any safe house.

Fortunately he was rarely ill, though he suffered from a heavy dose of influenza on Lestoquoi's farm. By then he knew of the French peasant's cure for the malady – a tumblerful of a mixture of equal parts of rum, honey and strong tea. This brew seemed to cure him within twenty-four hours. When he developed boils René Saublin gave him a course of injections of something Len did not bother to identify. 'Drop your trousers and bend over,' René said, and he threw a hypodermic needle at Len's buttocks as if tossing a dart into a target. When it failed to stick into the right place he said, 'Sorry, missed,' and tried again. After this he attached the syringe.

Len suffered his most violent sickness after eating pâté provided picnic style by one of his friends. The day was warm, and after a time and several helpings of pâté, he noticed that the mixture had become maggoty in the heat. For years afterwards the thought of that meal could make him instantly bilious.

Considering his difficult situation he generally ate well enough, though the official ration for the people of occupied northern France was meagre. Each person was entitled to one piece of meat a week, half a pound of rancid butter, and half a pound of coffee a month; the coffee content was slight, the mixture being mainly of powdered acorns and barley. Bread was not rationed and formed the staple diet; because the butter was so foul Len's friends sprinkled salt and pepper on it and dunked it in the acorn coffee. People with their own gardens had a reasonable quantity of vegetables and many bred fowls and rabbits. When Len stayed with farmers a supper of pâté and tripe was considered a satisfying meal, though after his unfortunate encounter with the picnic pâté Len gave it up for good.

Joseph Wiplier had made contact with an escape line operating from Lillers, near Bethune, which was said to be successful in passing prisoners and evaders right across France to the Pyrenees and then into Spain. Separate identity cards and passes were needed for each département crossed during the journey and somehow this group could provide all the necessary documentation.

Riding tandem, Len accompanied Joseph to Lillers to see the schoolmaster who was to be their contact, and in the interest of security they called at a cafe on the edge of town to make discreet inquiries. This was a wise precaution for the woman behind the bar told them that the teacher and his family had been arrested by the Gestapo the night before and that their screams of pain under torture could be heard all over the district.

The two men reflected, as they rode sadly home, that the Gestapo was having too many successes; Len's escape from 'Captain Evans' was one of their few defeats. His position was made more secure that afternoon when Marcelle Brien, the girl who specialised in providing identity papers, brought him a new card. His old identity as Leonard Masseux, aged twenty, had become dangerous as the Gestapo knew about it; his new card showed him as André Parsy, aged thirty-one, a coal miner. Coal miners were exempt from forced labour service in Germany. The photograph on the card showed Len with a drawn face and wearing a nasty scowl and he certainly looked ten years older than his real age.

In Lens a few nights later he had his first experience of an RAF bombing raid. It began with the German air-raid sirens, followed by the characteristic high-level thumps of anti-aircraft shells exploding. Then a solitary British pathfinder plane appeared to drop clusters of red, green and yellow parachute flares which were so bright that they lit up the whole town of Lens. Moments later the main bomber force arrived, their engines filling the air with thunderous noise. They had come to bomb the railway yards, which were virtually destroyed, but as always many French homes were hit and more than 100 townspeople were killed. Len was distressed and wondered how his friends would react to these deaths caused by the British. Without exception they said, in effect, 'It can't be helped; that's war.'

At this time Len was keeping on the move as much as possible so that the Gestapo would not be able to concentrate their attention on any one report of his having been sighted. He was in Lea Desmarais' house in La Bassée when somebody pressed the front door bell insistently. As he was on his own, Len would normally have ignored it but peeping through a curtain he saw Joseph Wiplier, looking worried and agitated, and let him in.

Without preamble, Joseph said, 'We're in trouble, Len. The Gestapo raided our house at six this morning – three carloads of them with two Alsation dogs. They know your name and that you use our house.'

This was bad news and it upset Len for he felt only a little less close to the Wiplier family than to the Faucomprez. Distressed, he sat down while Joseph told him of the morning's events. Joseph and his son Henri, fourteen, who had just started at the mines, were on night shift but Henri had finished earlier than his father and was having a bath when the Gestapo men smashed open the front door and burst in. Lucienne took this intrusion in her stride; with her hands on her hips she stood in the kitchen and eyed the Gestapo agents with innocent curiosity.

'Where is he?' the leader shouted.

'Who are you looking for?' Lucienne asked.

'That English pig Leonard. We know that he has been here.'
He noticed a coat hanging behind the door and sniffed it as if
trying to pick up an English scent – and the coat did indeed
belong to Len. 'Whose is this?' he demanded.

'It belongs to my husband,' Lucienne said mildly.

'Where is your husband?'

'He's at work in the mines on night shift and he won't be
back before eight p.m. I don't know who you are looking for
but you won't find him here.'

'No? We shall see. We know all about this English swine. Do
you know the punishment for people who help terrorists and
saboteurs?' He drew his finger across his throat. 'So! Kaput! We
finish them, all of them.'

Another German drew the leader's attention to an old radio
on a shelf. 'Switch it on!' he ordered Henri, who had come in
from the bathroom with a towel around his waist. The radio
screeched with the jamming which the Germans used in their
attempts to blot out BBC broadcasts.

'So you listen to radio London!' the German shouted. 'That is
forbidden.'

'No!' Henri exclaimed, panicking a little. 'Not London,
music. We listen to the music.' He pointed out that the radio
showed no names of transmitting stations and that he did not
know English; he only tuned in to music.

Before they left, the leader told Lucienne, 'Your husband will
report to Gestapo headquarters in Boulevard de la Liberté in Lille
at nine a.m. tomorrow morning.' He threw her a small card. 'He
will show that to the sentry on the door. He will not be late.'

Joseph was sure he had not been followed to La Bassée and
suspected that his sister-in-law, who disliked him, had sent the
Gestapo an anonymous letter but they were apparently not sure
that he had aided Len or they would have waited at the house
and arrested him. Len had been living with danger for a long
time and he was thinking clearly as he advised Joseph. 'Keep
your appointment with the Gestapo. Put on your best suit, wear
a trilby and look really smart; the Germans are impressed by a
well-dressed person. When the Gestapo agent questions you tell

him that you are president of the Annouellin football club [this was true] and that you have many visits from players and supporters. Perhaps one of them was mistaken for an Englishman. Give them the impression that you really want to co-operate.' He arranged to meet Joseph in Antoine Sion's cafe the following night to exchange news.

Deeply depressed at the thought of having brought possible disaster to the Wiplier family, Len left La Bassée and took the Lille road, turning off to Sainghan and passing the chateau, which had been taken over by a German infantry brigade. They spent hours each day practising landings from rafts on the chateau moat. Heavily preoccupied with worry over his friends, Len heard nothing unusual ahead of him – but then he cycled around a bend and found himself in the company of the German Army. An entire German infantry regiment in four separate companies took up the entire length of the road. This unwelcome sight was the beginning of one of the most extraordinary episodes of Len's career of evasion.

Too late to turn back without arousing suspicion, he rode on. There was just enough space for him to pass the first company by steering a very straight line. Some German soldiers jeered at him and one shouted 'Achtung! Der Englander!' As Len's heart missed a few beats the others laughed. This made Len feel better and he said to himself, 'All right, laugh you bastards! If you only knew!'

Len passed through the first three companies, each separated from the next by about twenty yards of road but found that the next company was in parade formation and in open order as they had taken up the whole road. A senior officer, who Len heard referred to as 'Herr Generale', was inspecting the troops. Len was not specially afraid in this situation; the men were clearly just ordinary soldiers, not SS storm troopers, and as a soldier himself he knew exactly what was going on. Unable to proceed, he stopped and sat astride his bike, cupped his hands and showed great interest in the proceedings. The general finished his inspection amid a flurry of salutes and 'Heil Hitlers!'

To Len's alarm, he then left the parade and with four officers behind him came towards the cyclist to reach the other companies. Len had rarely felt more conspicuous as the general gave him an icy smile and spoke to one of the officers. This man shouted an order – and Len jerked the bike in fright. But the officer was merely passing an order to the junior officer commanding the company; he saluted and in his turn shouted an order. With clicking jackboots the company closed ranks and then took two paces backwards, leaving a clear strip on the side of the road.

The general fixed his eyes on Len, gave him a warmer smile, and said very slowly in French with an atrocious and harsh accent, 'Allez, allez, vous pouvez passez.' (Go on, you can pass.)

Len did not at first comprehend, so the general said again, 'Allez, vous passez maintenant.'

Len now understood. The general had cleared the road so that he, Private Len Arlington of the Middlesex Regiment, could proceed. 'Merci, mon générale,' he said graciously and hoped that his voice was steady. Then, he slowly cycled past the German Army, the men standing rigidly to attention as if paying him a military courtesy.

'Very impressive parade, men,' he said softly in the manner of a British colonel. And he added, 'You stinking Boche.'

In his casual Cockney manner he winked at the last soldier in the line and then rode on, whistling cheerfully. He felt very satisfied about inspecting the German Army; his own army had never paid him such a compliment. Later, at the Sion Cafe, he told Amelie Sion about the episode and she passed it on to other Resistance people and everybody had a good laugh. Some of the men clapped Len on the back and said, 'Bravo, Lee-on-ar'! Bravo, Herr Generale Lee-on-ar'!'

It was a good day altogether, for Joseph had succeeded in deceiving the Gestapo. Following Len's advice, he was casual and compliant during the interview. When the Gestapo officer said that two men had been watching his home for some time and had seen a tall fair-haired young man aged about twenty entering, Joseph identified him as George, an Annoeullin footballer. Would the 'Herr Direktor' like to meet George? No, that would not be necessary but if Joseph learnt anything about the infamous Leonard he should report it at once; there was a good reward for information.

'Oh, of course, Herr Direktor,' Joseph said and added virtuously, 'Terrorists must be punished.'

'Thank you for your co-operation,' said the Gestapo chief, and Joseph almost smirked at him. He had also seen the letter which had denounced him, though he was not permitted to look at the handwriting. But he knew he was lucky and had come to the conclusion by the end of the interview that he had been dealt with by an officer of field police rather than Gestapo; a Gestapo man would not have been so easily satisfied.

That day had yet another surprise for Len. He spent the night with René and Mme Saublin and as they were drinking, Len sought René's reaction to an idea. 'Suppose I set off with a pitchfork over my shoulder and nothing else, and kept to the fields, how long would it take me to cross France and reach Spain?'

'Many months,' René said. 'Then you would have the mountains to cross. If you reached Spain the police would probably hand you back to the Germans. They don't like the British.'

'I might try it just the same,' Len said. 'I've got all the time in the world to make the trip.'

'Len, no!' René said decisively. 'We are going to need you soon and I have special orders from London for you.'

Len was incredulous. 'London knows that I am here?'

'Indeed yes. An agent from the War Office is in Lille at this very moment and has sent word that if you wish to join him he will be pleased to have you. The one thing he cannot do is get you back to England.'

The phony Captain Jack was still in Len's mind. 'How do you know this man is a genuine agent from London?'

'That's easy, he's an old friend of yours.' René laughed at Len's astonishment.

'I don't know anybody from the War Office,' Len objected.

'You are mistaken. I'll tell you a secret. This agent comes from your own regiment and he was billeted in Gondecourt. Your regiment was known as the forty-eighth because all your vehicles had a large forty-eight on the tail board.'

Len was still not satisfied. 'My regiment was infantry and the

secret service is not in the habit of withdrawing officers from
infantry units to parachute into France.'

René was insistent, Len hesitant. 'This is what we'll do,' Len
said. 'I'll put down my rank and number and details of my
service and names of people in the regiment and if he will do the
same I'll gladly throw in with him.' And this Len did on the spot.

'I'll see that he gets this,' René said. 'You are in for a great
surprise.'

Len doubted that he would be surprised. He knew that the
French loved romantic stories full of deceit and intrigue but he
had believed that the hard-headed René would know better
than to believe the British agent yarn. Meeting René a week
later, Len found him reserved and not his usual talkative self.
When Len pressed him for information about the British officer
René was apologetic. 'I'm sorry, Leonard, but his reply is that
for security he must break all contact with you.'

Len was not surprised. 'So he is just another Gestapo plant.
Don't you see, he can't take the risk of meeting me because I
would expose him.'

'Leonard', René said, 'it's not like that. When France is
liberated I'll make a point of fixing a rendezvous between you.
And by God, I'm going to enjoy the expression on your face
when you see him!'

René was telling Len the truth. The 'officer from the War
Office' was Michael Trotobas, promoted since Dunkirk to
captain, and now a key figure in the Resistance. He had judged
it too dangerous for Len to know about him, but as it happened
this was an error of judgment.

Though unable to tell Len anything about Trotobas, René
asked him to stay in the house for a few days as an important
member of the Resistance wanted to see him.

This man arrived the following evening and was introduced
as 'K.10' though his real name was Marcel Fertein and he was a
window-shutter maker in ordinary life. He was now in the
middle of an extraordinary life, posing as a police inspector and
with the identity card to prove it. A sharp-eyed, good-looking
man in his mid-thirties. Feretin asked Len many questions

about his connections and movements. Satisfied, he told the young soldier that from that moment he was a member of his own group, the *Réseau* Sylvestre Farmer, otherwise known as the 'War Office'. This was the group which Trotobas led and Fertein was his 'chief-of-staff' but he told Len nothing about Trotobas. He smoothed his dark hair, fingered his trim moustache and gave Len his orders: He was to stay in this part of France and gather information that might be useful to the group; he would pass it on to René, who would also relay any orders from 'K.10.'

When Fertein had departed, René said conspiratorially, 'We have a very special job for you on the day of liberation. You are the only man capable of doing the job, but I cannot give you any details yet.' And he refused to say any more.

Len spent a few days at La Bassée keeping out of sight while relaxing in a deck chair in Lea Desmarais' back garden and enjoying the brilliant sunshine. From that reclining position he heard an aircraft duel overhead but the planes were too far off for positive identification. A small red flash focussed his attention and out of the clear blue sky fell the two parts of a plane, apparently broken apart by an explosion. A fighter followed the wreckage down and Len now identified both planes – the fighter was a Messerschmidt 109, the destroyed plane a twin-engined American-made Boston bomber. Len ran for his bike and raced to the spot where it had fallen in a field two miles away.

A truckload of Nazi troops had beaten him to it and two officers were examining the smoking wreckage, amid which lay the corpses of the crew. A large and silent crowd had assembled and as they and Len watched, a remarkable incident occurred. Two French gendarmes cycled across the field, laid down their bikes and stood side by side as they adjusted their uniforms. Marching in step they approached the German officers and came to a halt as if about to salute them. Instead, they performed a precise military about-turn so that their backs were to the Germans. Then, still in unison, they saluted the dead Allied airmen. Ignoring the Germans, they performed another about-turn and returned to their bikes and slowly rode away as the crowd called 'Bravo, les gendarmes!'

Len felt encouraged by this small but impressive incident, as he did by other Allied air raids. The civilian losses, though, were grievous. A Spitfire attacked a train just outside La Bassée, missed it and hit a cottage, killing a six-year-old boy. Another Spitfire, mistaking a funeral cortège for a military convoy, killed many people among the mourners.

With a ceaseless need to concentrate and to remember details it was not surprising that sometimes Len had lapses of memory. One evening, en route to Lens, he remembered a few blocks from Lea Demarais's house that he had left his identity card there and hastened back to get it. As he fumbled to get his lock-pick into the keyhole a dozen gendarmes surrounded him and the officer in charge, the brigadier, threatened him with a pistol and demanded to know what he was doing.

Len was prepared to tell him but not in front of the entire La Bassée police force. 'If you would like to come inside for a moment I can explain who I am,' he said.

'Don't try hedging with me!' the brigadier said.

'I'm Belgian and I live here.'

'Then show me your identity card.'

Len knew that this police chief had a bad reputation for strong-arm tactics and that he had to bring Lea from the house, where she was still unaware of his predicament.

'Just come inside a moment and I will produce it,' he said desperately.

'I'll give you one minute,' the brigadier said, 'then I'll run you in.'

Len swung round and gave the bell-push a long press and as the brigadier knocked his hand away Lea appeared. 'Good evening brigadier,' she said sweetly, 'What's going on?'

'I want to see the identity of this young man who was entering your house.'

'But he's a nephew of mine from Belgium.'

'Then I would like to see his residence permit,' the brigadier insisted.

'Of course,' Lea agreed. 'Come in and I'll show it to you.' As the brigadier stepped inside he said to his men, 'Keep a close watch on him. Don't let him get away.'

Len came to a quick decision as he looked at these mostly young men. He would let them know who he was. He was sure that the brigadier would come out and order his arrest. Then he would run for it but he had to be sure that the gendarmes would act slowly. Turning to a big, blond young man who held him by the left arm he said, 'I want to warn you men that I am an escaped British soldier and the Germans have a price on my head. I cannot and will not allow myself to be arrested by French gendarmes and handed over to the Germans.'

The policemen stared at him. 'Why do you tell us this?' the blond gendarme asked.

'I want you to realise that I am not a common criminal. If your chief comes out and orders my arrest I will run − and trust to your patriotism to help me get away.'

They were silent and shuffled uneasily, until the brigadier came out. 'Very well, release him,' he said sourly while he glared at Len. 'His papers are quite in order.'

As Len went inside with Lea she said, 'He was going to run you in, no doubt of it. So I told him that I would denounce him after liberation and that I had plenty of witnesses to back me up.' She smiled wickedly. 'So he changed his mind.'

The following night the young blond gendarme arrived with a cake for Len, baked by his wife, as well as some provisions put together by some of his colleagues. 'Lord, you had a nerve last night!' he said. 'Telling us you wouldn't be arrested by a dozen gendarmes! I believe you would have fought the lot of us.'

Len just grinned, but he would have fought had his wits failed. The episode had turned out well; he now had friends in the La Bassée police force and they could be counted on for a warning if the Gestapo planned to raid a house.

He had another narrow escape only a few days later in Annoeullin, where the coalminers had been on strike; it was their contribution to sabotaging the German war effort as their coal was sent to Germany. After the strike had lasted a week German troops ringed the town with only three yards between men. Other troops carried out a house-to-house search and demanded identity cards; every man whose occupation was shown as miner was pushed into a collecting truck. Len was trapped in the cafe Sion as the searching troops approached and Amelie Sion said urgently, 'Quick, Leonard, into the Germans' hall behind the café!' The place was no longer a barracks and as Amelie had the key she locked Len in. Soldiers tried the door violently and seemed about to break it down until Amelie drew their attention to the big sign which proclaimed in German, ENTRITT VERBOTTEN. 'Soldaten Deutsche,' Len heard her say. It was enough; the troops went away.

It was a bad day for Annoeullin. Nearly every family in the town lost somebody, all carried off nobody knew where, without spare clothing or food. For Len, the worst blow of all was that they took Henri Wiplier, one of the youngest of all the miners. His parents were distraught for they believed, like the relations of all the other seized men, that the Germans might shoot the miners as an example to all the miners of France. For weeks after they were taken nobody knew what had happened to them. In fact, they were taken to a concentration camp in Holland, and here subjected to treatment designed to break their spirit. First their heads were shaven, then they were put into huts from which all window glass had been removed. They slept in wooden bunks with only one blanket each and during the day were kept standing on parade in icy winds and snow; during particularly bad weather the Nazis made them strip in the cold, and some older men died from exposure and pneumonia. The food ration was just enough to keep a man alive. The miners endured six months of this 'punishment' before being returned to Annoeullin – and Henri Wiplier was among them. They did not again go on strike. The Nazis knew how to force most of the French people away from ideas of Resistance.

12

'NINE SWALLOWS FELL FROM THE SKY'

Len returned to La Bassée while Annoeullin was in a state of turmoil. He needed a haircut and had been told of a woman barber who, it was said, cut a man's hair without asking too many questions. He found her hut in a hidden-away part of the town and told the woman how he would like his hair cut. 'You aren't French?' she asked.

'Polish,' Len said. 'And you?'

'French and proud of it.'

Len let the conversation die. He had to be careful what nationality he adopted whenever it was necessary to explain his slight non-French accent. To call himself Belgian often proved a mistake for people would burst into a torrent of Flemish; many Flemish Belgians spoke no French.

Another customer came in and started a conversation with the woman barber. Len, in a comfortably relaxed state, took no notice until he heard the man say in a pregnant tone of voice, 'Last night the swallows fell from the sky.'

The woman, after a pause, said, 'How many?'

'Nine American swallows. We don't know what to do with them yet.'

Len sighed in despair. He did not need to be a Resistance man to decipher this transparent message. For all these two conspirators knew he was a collaborator, even a Gestapo agent, and they could at least have been patient until they were alone before talking about nine shot-down American airmen. He hurried to Annoeullin to pass the news to René Saublin, so that

Marcel Fertein could be told; nine American airmen would be a fine haul for the Gestapo and they must be moved quickly.

Shut up in a house in La Bassée nine airmen would quickly draw attention to themselves. Everybody engaged in Resistance work knew that airmen were the biggest risk of all evaders. They talked too much and too loudly and they seemed to have no self-discipline. One woman in the district had given sanctuary to two airmen for whom the Germans were searching. She put them in an upstairs room and told them to be silent and still, should anybody call at the front door. A Nazi officer arrived with a patrol to search houses in her street but the woman, a level-headed nurse, managed to convince him that she was above suspicion. The officer was in the process of leaving when he heard footsteps moving backwards and forwards on the floor above. He glanced at the nurse, who said calmly, 'My parents from the country.'

'Parents with a marching footstep, Madame?' the officer said with a grim smile. Pistol in hand, he ran upstairs and returned with the shamefaced airmen. Tense and nervous, one of them had started to prowl about the room. His inability to remain still put a brave woman into a concentration camp. Rashness and thoughtlessness among servicemen had been responsible for many deaths among the people trying to help them. Such behaviour made Len very angry and sharply aware of the danger posed by even one evader let alone nine in a group.

René sent Len back to La Bassée to find out where the airmen were in hiding. When he met Lea he was not too surprised when she said, 'How would you like to meet some American airmen?' As he had feared, the word was spreading. Somebody had suggested that Lea should take Len to their hiding place as nobody else could speak to the men in English.

The house was a small, red-bricked building near the railway station and as Lea rang the door bell they both heard a mad scampering of feet and banging of doors – exactly like nine careless men charging for cover. 'Oh God!' Len said. 'How many people will this bunch kill if we can't get them away quickly?'

The door was opened by a strongly built man in his forties,

wearing riding breeches, gaiters and a black beret. He was, he said, Maurice Bouchery. Lea pushed herself past him and identified herself and Len, and Bouchery called 'O.K.'

A dark, good-looking young woman, Madame Tetard, and nine young men in a motley assortment of clothing, filed into the room. Bouchery started to explain to them about the visitors and then, embarrassed, deferred to Len.

'I'm an escaped British prisoner of war,' Len told them, 'and I'm sorry to meet you under these conditions. If there is anything I can do for you, let me know.'

A short, dark man stepped forward with hand outstretched. 'Are we pleased to meet you, Limey. We don't understand a word these Froggies keep jabbering about.'

The men were taking turns to sleep and even to eat and the senior officer said they were already 'going nuts'. He was aware, he said, that their presence was a strain on the people of the house. Len was even more concerned than the captain. He knew that the nine would have to be split up and got into the country but it was a big job and organisation was needed. Bikes had to be procured and the men moved in groups of no more than three.

'I can arrange to get you out of here and onto an escape line,' he told the captain. 'But it's not something I can do quickly, not this minute. You will have to keep your men still, quiet and away from the windows.'

'Do you guys hear that?' the captain said. 'Our Limey friend wants you to clam up – and that's an order from me too.' The men nodded but Len had no great confidence in them. 'I mean it,' he insisted. 'If the Gestapo gets just a whisper than airmen are here you will finish up in the bag and these people will get the chop.' He drew his hand across his throat.

'Sure, sure,' the American said. 'We'll be good.'

Len hurried away to talk with Rene Saublin and between them they decided that the safest place for the moment was the nearest isolated house – that of the farmer Lestoquoi. Len pedalled fast to Lestoquoi and made the arrangements, though Lestoquoi was reluctant to be involved, and then organised bike transport. When he returned to René the older man gave him an unhappy grimace and spread his hands in a gesture of despair. 'I've just had a message, Len,' he said. 'The Gestapo have caught the Americans and they've arrested Bouchery and Madame Tetard.'

'We couldn't have moved any faster, René,' Len said helplessly.

It was time for the friends to separate for a time until the inevitable Gestapo round-up was over. Somebody at the house in La Bassée would have mentioned the presence of an escaped British soldier, and the Gestapo would at once know that he was 'the Englander schweinhund Leonard' they were so desperate to capture.

M. Bouchery paid the penalty for the lack of discipline among the Americans and his failure to keep their presence secret; he died facing a firing squad. His execution was a blow to the morale of the people of La Bassée but a much greater reverse depressed the patriotic people of all France. The BBC broadcast news of the British and Canadian commando raid on Dieppe on August 19, 1942. 'After inflicting heavy losses on the German garrison in the Dieppe region our troops carried out their withdrawal as planned,' the BBC announcer said. This euphemism for defeat fooled nobody with any military sense or knowledge, and the extent of the disaster was soon common knowledge in France. The British and Canadians had lost nearly 2,000 dead and another 2,200 had been taken prisoner. That they had killed 600 Germans did not make the venture into a triumph.

The announcer's defiant 'Courage, mes amis, nous les aurons les boches!'* on the day of the battle did nothing to raise morale. René, listening to the radio with Len, said bitterly. 'It's all right for him to be talking about getting the Boche in the end but we've got the bastards right now and we could do without them.' He knew, as did Len, that after the Dieppe disaster the invasion of Europe would be deferred for at least a year, and probably longer.

* 'Courage, my friends, we'll get the Boche in the end.'

With such a long wait inevitable, Len decided on a more permanent hideout. He and Paul, Lea's son, dug a hole 10 feet deep, 10 feet long and 5 feet wide in Lea's garden, which was hidden from her neighbours. Into the hole they lowered an iron single bed and covered the hole with planks which Paul had salvaged from a sunken canal barge, leaving a square hole for entry. Four feet of earth covered the boards while the entrance was concealed with a box in which grew flowers and grass over the hideout itself. They ran in a concealed cable for light and two air vents were hidden in clusters of flowers. This was to be Len's sleeping-quarters for the next two years, whenever he stayed at Lea's house. He slept more easily there, confident that he was safe unless the Gestapo put sniffer dogs into the garden.

In December 1942 good news came from Gondecourt – Fi-Fi had been released from prison. Len asked Lea to make contact and this brave, resolute and energetic woman did not demur. She returned that night with news that she had arranged for Fi-Fi to spend a weekend with her at La Bassée – and she would bring her daughters. Lea lived only five minutes' walk from the station but she took her visitors on a circuitous two-mile route so that they could reach her home undetected. Len enjoyed that weekend more than any for years because he had again the deep satisfaction of being part of a family. They all spoke of the absent Pierre, who was getting letters through to Fi-Fi but not once did he hint at the terrible time he was enduring in the German concentration camp.

Marcelle and Len, very much in love, made a secret arrangement so that they could correspond with each other. Jo-Jo, Joseph Wiplier's son, was working in the same factory as Marcelle and he became their go-between. It might have been a dangerous arrangement but the letters were never signed and no open reference was made to other people. Had the Gestapo found and read the letters nobody would have been incriminated.

Throughout 1943 Len was busy with Resistance business, reporting to his chief, Marcel Fertein, through René Saublin, though occasionally he met Fertein personally. He supplied information about German movements in the region south and south-east of Lille and passed on the names of men and women who might safely be approached to work for the Resistance. Len's manner, as well as his status as an English escaped prisoner, induced people to confide in him and Fertein regarded him as the best informed of all his agents.

Some great Resistance actions of the war did not become known because both the Germans and the Resistance often had good reasons for keeping them secret, but occasionally a grand coup of sabotage became general knowledge. One such operation took place during June, 1943.

The Chiefs of Staff in London wanted the French locomotive works at Fives, Lille, to be destroyed. It was one of the most important plants in Western Europe and British and American planes had tried to knock it out, but the approaches to Lille were defended by the Germans' heaviest anti-aircraft defences in northern France and no direct hit had been scored.

At a conference in London the Chiefs of Staff asked the SOE representative, Brigadier Mockler-Ferryman, if his agents could do the job. He put the question to Michael Trotobas. In a way Trotobas had his mind made up for him by what the people of Lille were enduring. In their gallant efforts to bomb the railway sheds the pilots were dropping bombs on working-class districts and casualties among civilians were mounting.

Trotobas radioed that he would take out the Fives works. After much preparation, he put his plan into effect on the night of June 26/27. About nineteen men in all were involved but only the spearhead group penetrated into the giant factory. A German-speaker posed as a Nazi colonel, while Trotobas himself was 'Police Inspector Dulard'. Obtaining entry by a superb piece of bluff – to search for terrorists who were trying to blow up the plant – Trotobas and his men placed twenty-four magnet explosive charges on key machinery. Then they went to the cafe Aquarium and waited for the explosions. The tremendous blasts destroyed twenty-two transformers and a fire caused much other damage.

Trotobas' message to London – 'Mission successful' was received by the Air Staff with scepticism. They told the SOE 'Tell your man to send photographs of the operation area.'

Getting photographs was more difficult than planting bombs. The factory was crawling with Gestapo, Army officers, SS guards and French police. But Trotobas returned to the scene armed with a forged pass which described him as a senior inspector of a major insurance company and told the senior SS colonel in charge that his company needed photographs of the damage if it was to pay out millions of francs in compensation.

The colonel, being an orderly minded German, saw the logic of this and ordered soldiers to hold lights while Trotobas photographed the ruins. The pictures were sent to a British Intelligence drop station in Normandy and then across the channel. When the RAF officers opened the package they found a small card – *With the compliments of the Resistance.*

The Germans posted a reward of one million francs for the 'British terrorist' and two informers worked their way into his *réseau* but Trotobas suspected them and they were made to talk and to confess. Their bodies were dumped at the back entrance of the Gestapo HQ in Rue Leon Gambetta, Lille, each with a label, *With the compliments of the Resistance.*

Trotobas' sabotage expert was 'Olivier', a British Army officer, who when in Arras lived with the family of a baker, a Resistance man. Olivier was too fond of talking about his exploits and this invited Gestapo attention. Agents caught him in a raid on the baker's house and under torture he revealed Trotobas' address – 20 Boulevard de Belfort – though he had every reason to believe that his chief would not be at that house at that time. Early in the morning of November 23, 1943 the Gestapo and the Army trapped Trotobas in the house, with his girlfriend and collaborator, Denise Gilman. Both died in the consequent shoot-out. The Germans made great propaganda capital out of Trotobas' death, which was widely reported in the press in northern France, but everybody knew that he had done much damage to the Nazis' war effort.

Trotobas was a fine Resistance man in every particular but one – he had not cultivated safe houses in the way that Len Arlington had done. Len would never have used No. 20 Boulevard de Belfort. It was set on the corner of two streets of tenement houses, all of which had high walls at the back. The only way out was through the front door and the building did not even have a skylight.

At that time Len still did not know the identity of the SOE officer in Lille, but he heard about the torture inflicted on 'Olivier' – the Germans had 'jumped on his toes'. Among Resistance men this was considered mild treatment and their bitter feeling was that 'Olivier' should have died rather than betray his chief. Len was disappointed that he had not been allowed to meet the officer from his own battalion, but René Saublin, as he had promised, passed to Marcel Fertein the slip of paper on which Len had written his army details. When Fertein gave it to Trotobas he said, 'Good God! Young Arlington!'

He was silent for a while, weighing instructions from London to avoid contact with all British soldiers, against his own judgment on this particular British soldier, whom he trusted. Then he said, 'Whatever happens, K.10, this young man and I must never come face to face.'

'Is he dangerous?'

'Not at all. He's a good soldier with a lot of common sense.'

'That's the way he seems to me,' Fertein agreed. 'He has a real sense for security and everybody says he is the only British soldier in the whole district who hasn't caused a lot of trouble. René Saublin tells me that his judgment is cool and he doesn't panic. So can I use him in the group?'

'By all means,' Trotobas said. 'But just make sure that he and I never meet.'

The order from his London superiors was designed to ensure that Trotobas could not be given away by somebody, while under torture, who had known him in the British Army. Len was the only person in France who knew his real name, though a photograph exists which shows Trotobas, in civilian clothes, with Yvonne Passy, daughter of the Resistance leader Madame Passy. Perhaps Trotobas was inclined to make personal contact with Len. Had he done so then almost certainly he would have learnt something about the use of safe houses – and this knowledge could have kept him alive.

Len was annoyed with Fertein, holding him responsible for not being permitted to know of Trotobas, and after the war he refused to speak to him for five years. His bitterness was overcome when he learnt that Trotobas was following orders given to him in London and that Fertein himself was following Trotobas' orders.

Fertein himself had a narrow escape from capture. Trotobas' replacement, Georges Bayard, called him to a meeting in the Cafe Scoufflers, Lille, with Jean Vandeneeckhoutts, a leading Resistance man. As they sat at a table, Gestapo agents rushed in, covering them with revolvers. After searching each of the men they produced handcuffs, at which point Bayard made a dash for the back door. He was shot down but his brave attempt at escape gave Fertein a chance to run out of the front door and he raced off on his bike.

Len, like every other Resistance worker, learned to anticipate some dangers but some came not only unannounced and unexpectedly but also in unforeseeable ways. Among his safe houses was one owned by Albert and Rose Dupon, in the mining town of Bethune. The house was safe but the Dupons' daughter was a walking booby trap. A promiscuous girl, she had a quick interest in anything that wore trousers. Len knew her reputation and did nothing more than smile at her because he understood the risks involved if he should run foul of jealous boyfriends. In fact, Mademoiselle Dupon had a fiancé, which made her even more dangerous.

One day her parents were out and she and Len were left alone. Len stayed cool despite the girl's provocative postures and was sitting reading when her fiancé's mother, who lived next door, walked in. The situation was innocent but the woman chose to see it as compromising; at that time and in that society a 'nice' girl was not left unchaperoned with a man. That evening the fiancé, Pierre, a coal miner, stamped into the house and demanded that the girl return all his presents. Even worse, he threatened to denounce the whole family for having sheltered a British escaped prisoner. Then, still angry, he stalked out.

Len did not take his threat seriously until Albert Dupon, who followed the young man out of the house, returned in great agitation to say that Pierre was indeed heading for town. Len gave chase. Pierre was fit and a good runner and he sprinted a mile through the crowded streets with Len pounding behind him. A former regimental running champion, Len brought Pierre low with a flying rear tackle just 200 yards short of the German town headquarters, twisted his arm into a hammerlock and marched him home. Hundreds of peope had seen this mad chase but, for once, neither French nor German police were on the streets. Much later Pierre thanked Len for not mentioning his threat of denunciation; it would have been enough, in 1945, to have had him shot for collaboration.

Mademoiselle Dupon did not reform. On another occasion Len was in her company with two other young men, a situation he considered safe enough. The four were playing cards and the girl and the other men started to giggle and become flushed. For a while Len thought they were laughing at him and he was puzzled. When the other three lost all concentration on the game and became agitated he looked under the table. Mlle. Dupon's shoes were on the floor and she had her left leg full length up the trousers of one young man and her right leg was similarly engaged in the trousers of the other man. It was an easy enough manoeuvre in the wide, full-bottomed trousers of the time.

After that Len moved on; the Dupon house was anything but safe. It would be safer, he reflected, living next to Gestapo Headquarters.

13

'THE IDEAL MAN FOR THE JOB'

No matter how hard they tried, the Nazis could not impose an information blackout on occupied France. Listening to the BBC was a serious offence but many people did listen and what they heard they passed on. Len and his friends were heartened by the news of the Allied landings in Sicily and Italy and the Luftwaffe's 'Little Blitz' on London – Operation Steinbock, January 21, 1944 – was not too worrying. Len was fortunate in that he had no family back home to worry about, a factor which deeply depressed many prisoners in German hands.

It was known in France that the British and Americans were heavily bombing German cities – and the French applauded this destruction. The Bishop of Chichester questioned the morality of RAF 'area bombing' raids on German cities. A Government spokesman, Viscount Cranbourne, replied in the House of Lords that the Government was 'prepared to bring the whole life of the German cities to a standstill in order to paralyse enemy production.' It was an attitude the French understood. The RAF badly damaged the great Dunlop factory at Montluçon, France; when the Germans repaired it the Resistance crippled it again.

In many parts of France the Nazis, reacting to the Allied invasion, were behaving with appalling savagery and on the night of April 1, 1944, it was the town of Ascq, in Len's district, which suffered. Three Resistance men, Lelong, Marge and Delecluse, laid a charge on the Brussels–Lille railway line near Ascq to blow up a German troop train, carrying the Armoured Reconnaissance battalion of the 12th SS Panzer Division. The charge went off about 10.30 p.m. and two wagons were derailed, without causing casualties to the Germans. All was calm until it was reported that shots had been fired at the train from nearby houses, though it is doubtful if this really happened.

An SS officer, Lieut. Hauck, overreacted. Ordering his men, fully-armed, from the train, he shouted, 'The miserable French have dared to raise their hand against elite troops of Adolf Hitler! The village will now pay the price!'

And it did. The SS butchers broke into houses and cafes, searching for hostages and victims, all the time firing machine guns and machine pistols through windows and doors. Many people were dragged from their beds and, viciously bashed and bayoneted, they were forced towards the railway station. Several women were beaten bloody by squads of SS thugs.

That night the SS massacred 86 people; their youngest victim was 15 and the oldest 76. The line was repaired by 2 a.m. on April 2 and before the train left an officer shouted, 'Next time one of our trains is sabotaged we will burn the town to the ground!' It was a Sunday morning and some of the shocked survivors stumbled to the church – to find that the vicar and curate had been murdered and mutilated.

With remarkable rapidity, the BBC reported the atrocity the same morning and Len, with Amelie Sion and others, heard about it at Annoeullin, only ten miles away. Len, who was usually mild-mannered, even when talking about the Germans, was as white with anger and shock as any of his French friends. All dearly wanted vengeance against the barbarians who had savaged Ascq.

On Saturday, May 20, the French – and Belgians – were acutely aware of the scale of the Allied air attacks on military targets; 5,000 aircraft destroyed twelve rail targets and nine airfields in France and Belgium.

The Resistance became increasingly active and by the end of May Len was encouraging his friends with his belief that an Allied offensive was likely during the early summer. From where he stood, the Germans had been sufficiently softened up for an invasion to take place. He knew, as other Resistance men did, that all the groups had orders to carry out particular acts of sabotage when the long-awaited invasion began.

He spent the night of June 5, 1944, at Amelie Sion's cafe and she woke him excitedly next morning with the news that the BBC had announced a great landing in Normandy. Already people had gathered in her cafe where they were listening to the radio and talking about the battles likely to follow the invasion. Instructions from London to the French people stressed the need for caution. Above all, they should not provoke the Germans in brutal reprisals. In Annoeullin this made sense to most people; they were still horrified by the massacre at Ascq.

For his first visit that day Len called on René Saublin, who was clad as ever in his white blouse and black beret. He greeted Len effusively. 'I am so glad to see you, Leonard; we were just talking about you.'

In the sitting room were two other men of Annoeullin, members of René's group, and Len was introduced. 'Sit down, Leonard,' René said, with even more than his usual affability. 'We were just running through that job we want you to do for us. You remember I told you about a very special job after liberation?' He turned to the others. 'Leonard is the ideal man for the job. Being British, nobody will be able to lay a hand on him.'

So it's a raid, Len thought; we're going to attack the Germans in Seclin or perhaps we are going to shoot up Gestapo headquarters. He would like that.

'The target won't be able to run for it,' René said laughing. 'His car, which is in Pruvost's garage, has been taken care of. The wire running from the coil to the distributor has been removed and replaced by a dummy wire so he will have a real job starting it up.' This amused all three men. René dug a finger into Len's chest. 'This is where you come in, my dear friend. We will provide you with a loaded revolver' – he spoke in the tone of a man announcing a prize for a lucky contest winner – 'and as soon as you know exactly where he is you will fill him full of lead. You will be our executioner.' His tone was dramatic.

Len was not too happy about this proposition. He liked the

idea of killing Germans in a fight or even in field ambush but cold-blooded assassination did not appeal to him. 'Who is this unlucky victim?' he asked.

'Why, Henri Dal, the mayor, of course!' René said. 'I thought you would have guessed that.'

'The mayor!' Len was appalled. 'The mayor of Annoeullin? Why should you want him dead?'

'He's a collaborator. Everybody knows that.'

'I don't know it,' Len said. He was beginning to suspect a plot to dispose of the mayor using the Resistance as a cover. Why should René, who was not even French, want to kill him? Murdering a defenceless French civilian was not Len's idea of war. 'Tell me exactly what you are accusing him of,' he demanded. 'Unless you can give me proof that he has knowingly caused the death of at least one Resistance member I cannot carry out your order.'

'He's a collaborator,' René repeated, 'and that should be proof enough. All the principal citizens of Annoeullin have demanded that he be shot as a traitor.'

'Then get the citizens of Annoeullin to carry out the execution,' Len suggested. 'I can't go around shooting Frenchmen unless they shoot at me.'

René was disappointed and annoyed but he spoke patiently, 'Look Leonard,' he said, 'you don't have to be afraid of the consequences. You have the full support of the French Resistance behind you.'

Len shook his head firmly, 'I'm sorry, René, nothing doing. I am a British soldier and I cannot shoot Frenchmen without having to answer for it when the war is over. I am certain that Captain Fertein would never give me such an order.'

Now René lost his patience. 'Captain Fertein told you to take orders from me!' he snapped. 'You were there when he said so.'

'Not that type of order,' Len said. 'Get him down here and we can talk it over.' He knew that René would not stop arguing and cajoling so he stood up. 'We will continue the discussion once Captain Fertein is here.' Then he wished them good luck and walked out, disillusioned with René and his ideas of what the Resistance stood for.

He was interested in obtaining arms to fight the Germans now that the allied invasion had come, and when he returned to the Wiplier house he found that Joseph had the same idea. He had brought from hiding a very old rifle with a very long barrel, rather like something from the backwoods of eighteenth-century Canada. He had just five cartridges for the gun. 'Well, it's something to start with,' Len said encouragingly, 'but don't go to war until I give the order. Please don't.'

Jo-Jo Wiplier came in from work with a note from Marcelle, asking Len to come to Chemy early on Sunday as they had received news of Pierre. After spending the evening at Sion Cafe, Len left soon after three a.m., taking a risk on meeting a curfew patrol as he crossed through Annoeullin. Just after four a.m. he crawled through the Faucomprez back garden to find Fi-Fi and the girls waiting for him.

The 'news' of Pierre was less exciting than Len had hoped for. It was nothing more than that Fi-Fi had had a premonition. On waking up the previous morning, she had told Marcelle with quiet but total conviction, 'Papa will be home tomorrow.'

'Well, that's something to hope for,' Len told her tactfully, but he was disappointed.

'It is obvious,' Fi-Fi said, 'that as Pierre's last letter was three months ago he is now on his way home.'

'I'm afraid that all mail has been delayed because of Allied bombing,' Len explained patiently. 'The whole of Germany must be in a chaotic state.'

'Pierre will be home today,' Fi-Fi said again.

Len shrugged, gave the two girls a look of resignation and settled down reluctantly to a day of hopeless waiting, since Fi-Fi obviously wanted him to stay. Len was deeply in love with Marcelle and under normal circumstances he would have been happy to stay in Chemy just to be with her. But this house was dangerous and he was continually tense; Marcelle could feel his tension every time she held his hand.

By nightfall he was uneasy. The last time he had spent a night in this house the Germans had arrived to arrest him. Next time they came there would be no getting away over the roof. Next

time, too, these three women would be executed. He loved
them dearly – too dearly to remain.

'Please stay, just for one night,' Fi-Fi begged him. 'I know that
he will return. Please, Leonard.'

Len gave in. 'All right,' he said, 'but I will keep watch all
night. I will never be able to sleep soundly in this house again.'
He kept observation from his bedroom window, the window
from which he had seen the Germans come hunting him three
years before. He opened the window onto a very dark moonless
night, and reflected on the possible course of the war from
now on. The Allies would win, that was obvious, but at great
cost. The invading armies were still a long way off and this part
of France could become a battleground. The Germans in the
district had not eased the pressures of occupation and he did
not propose to relax his guard.

A dog barked in the distance. A second dog joined in. Within
five minutes every dog in Chemy was barking and Len's scalp
prickled in apprehension. He was soon certain that someone
was reconnoitring outside. As he heard footsteps he shut the
window and called quietly and urgently to Fi-Fi, 'Come
quickly! There is someone prowling around.'

Fi-Fi was with him in seconds and they saw a dark form in
the street, peering up at the window. He stopped, gathered
loose shingle and threw it at the window panes. With that Fi-Fi
screamed, 'It's Papa! Marcelle! Jervaise! It's Papa outside!' And
the women went running.

Len hesitated. He was agonisingly aware that he had been the
cause of Pierre's imprisonment. How would Pierre feel about
him now? He had every right to be resentful. Walking quietly
and slowly down the stairs Len heard Pierre's first anxious
words as he entered his home. 'Is Leonard all right? He hasn't been
caught, has he?'

Len wept at that. And he was weeping as he embraced the
older man, who hugged him and said, 'Ah, how happy I am to
see everybody is here; nobody is missing.'

The Germans had freed him on the day the Allies landed in
Normandy; they drove him to the German-Belgian frontier and

dumped him. He had suffered terribly in prison – though he kept much of this from his family that night – and he had lost most of his hair and much of his normal weight. His hand on Len's shoulder, he said, 'I was very glad that I had to go through it and not you, Leonard. As a prisoner of the Germans in the last war I got used to their harsh treatment.'

When they had talked until three a.m. Fi-Fi switched on the kitchen light, saying, 'I'll make some fresh coffee and then we can get some rest.'

As the kettle came to the boil two rifle shots cracked in the back yard and all four people started up in fear. Fi-Fi switched off the light, Pierre bolted the door and they ran upstairs to peer through a window and see what was happening. Six Germans stood in the garden, staring at the house with their rifles at the ready.

'They must have followed you, Pierre,' Len hissed.

'Impossible. They're a passing patrol attracted by the kitchen lights. If they were more than that they wouldn't have fired warning shots. They would have come in.'

A German tried to see through the kitchen window, which Fi-Fi, in the general excitement, had that evening forgotten to cover with its blackout blind. The tension in the house was almost palpable, Len reflecting on the dreadful irony of being captured on Pierre's first night of freedom at home. The women were taut with fear and even Pierre held his breath. If Len were caught in his house now. . . . After a while the soldiers departed arguing and their footsteps faded away. Len had been lucky once again, but he did not stretch his luck and left Chemy at daybreak, returning to Annouellin where Joseph had obtained another rifle. They set to work to clean them.

The fighting was getting closer to northern France as the German line was pushed back by the advancing Allies and all Resistance men were oiling their firearms as they waited for their chance to attack isolated or left-behind groups of Germans or stragglers. Tactics were planned and targets were debated and there was a tendency to forget that the German Army was still extremely powerful and full of fight.

On August 31, 1944, the British crossed the Somme and captured Amiens, while the Americans crossed the Meuse, near Sedan; next day the British reached Arras and the Americans occupied Verdun. That night Len left Annoeullin for Chemy. One object of his trip was to be sure that the Faucomprez family were prepared for the inevitable difficulties which would follow when two great armies moved in conflict across the region. His decision to travel via the canal was dangerous because the Resistance had recently blown up the sluice gates of one of the locks to prevent barges from taking coal to Germany. The Germans had posted guards on either side of the locks; also, knowing that the saboteurs had arrived on bikes along the towpath, they had put tractors in the way. In the dark, Len braked only just in time to avoid smashing into a tractor and as he half jumped, half fell from the saddle a German soldier came out of the darkness and his pointing rifle and bayonet showed that he meant business.

'Halte!' he shouted.

With the bayonet point inches from his throat Len slowly raised his hands.

'Papiers?' the German demanded.

Len carefully lowered one hand and withdrew his identity card and handed it over.

The German studied it, flashed a lamp in Len's face and asked a question in German.

'Nix compris,' Len said, using a phrase common among the French when questioned by a German, to show that they did not understand. But Len well understood what the question was likely to be – 'What are you doing here during curfew?' To be out between ten p.m. and six a.m without special German papers was forbidden, and cycling along the canal towpath was absolutely prohibited. Len was in another fix.

'Komme mit,' the German said, and covering Len with his rifle motioned him to a guard hut. A shout brought a second soldier to the door and Len saw two others playing cards inside. The second man questioned Len, also in German, and both eyed him with deep suspicion. It was time for some play-acting.

Looking very worried by screwing his forehead into a frown, Len said pleadingly, 'Compris? Piccaninny malade! Moi chercher doctor, compris? Bébé krank, malade, sick. Moi, je vais searcher le doctor.' He tried to emphasise the German pronunciation of doctor – 'dok-tor'.

The Germans talked this over and the word 'doktor' kept cropping up. Whenever one of the Germans uttered the word Len said quickly, 'Yah, Herr Dok-tor'. And when they glanced at him he looked anxious and sighed heavily in distress. Finally, the sentry returned his identity card and muttered, 'Schnell! Schnell! Raus!'

A few years before, during the prisoners' march, Len had become accustomed to this command to move smartly, so he said, 'Merci, danke', and raced off.

For once, Len's main purpose in visiting Chemy was not to see the Faucomprezs; he wanted to collect a rifle and ammunition promised to him long before by M. Salomez, the secretary at the Chemy town hall. In the Faucomprez house, he handed Len a short-barrelled cavalry carbine in excellent condition, with fifteen rounds of ammunition. 'I would like to have a few shots at the Boche myself,' he said regretfully, 'but I am a little too old for that. I'm sure you will make a better job of it than I could. Good luck and good hunting!'

For many Frenchmen the tracking down and killing of German soldiers was assuming the proportions of the hunt – with the most dangerous animals of all as the quarry.

A rifle has a tell-tale shape even when wrapped in an old potato sack and carried across a bike's handlebars but this was how Len took the carbine back to Annoeullin, which was full of German soldiers, and laid it with Joseph's weapons under the tiles of an outhouse.

About twelve Spitfires were circling overhead, apparently looking for a worthwhile target. When Joseph's son came running with the news that a German troop train had stopped at Annoeullin railway station Joseph prayed that the Spitfires would drop bombs on it. Len said sadly, 'No such luck; these planes are fighters and don't carry bombs.'

His knowledge was a little out of date. At that moment four of the planes came diving in with engines screaming and a huge oblong object, the spare fuel tank, fell away from the lead plane. Then it dropped a big bomb, the green and yellow circles painted on its nose clearly visible. The planes were after the troop train but only one bomb landed near it. It caused no casualties but it did hold up the train.

Excited and wanting action himself, Len rode to Carnin to see a friend who had organised his own small Resistance group, a retired miner named Jean-Baptiste Dievart. Small, very thin and in his fifties, he was nevertheless enthusiastic and he shouted a welcome to Len. 'We need you! You must stay and give us support in case the Germans from the train make a run for it! They must come this way if they are heading for Lille – and we will be waiting.'

Len looked round at Dievart's fighters and considered that he was a trifle overambitious. His force numbered three. One was armed with a revolver, while Clotaire Durot, aged seventeen, had a sawn-off shotgun and only two cartridges. But there was a problem about this weapon. Normally the barrel of a shotgun is sawn off, making it easier to hide and deadly at close range, but Durot had sawn off the butt. He demonstrated to Len how he could slide the weapon under the trouser belt and down the leg of his trousers. Len stared at the extraordinary weapon in amazement, for now it could neither be held properly nor fired accurately. 'Never fire that thing,' he said firmly.

'Oh, why not?' the youth asked.

'Well, never mind,' Len said. 'Just shove it down your trousers.' He turned to the third man. 'And where's your gun?'

'I'm waiting for one of these two to get shot and I'll take over his gun,' he said.

'Crikey, Jean-Baptiste,' Len said worriedly, 'you're going to fight Gernmans with these chaps and these weapons?'

'My men are formidable.' Dievart retorted. He was in no mood for criticism.

'Absolutely bloody terrifying,' Len said in English. He took them out to a small field behind Dievart's house and set them in long grass overlooking the Annoeullin road. They were well hidden and could see what passed on the road, a good hundred yards away, and perhaps they could pick off an isolated soldier.

In the distance was heavy gunfire, a sign that the Allied armies were approaching from the south. More immediately, also approaching was a German horse-drawn wagon coming from Annoeullin. Four Germans sat in it, one driving with a comrade beside him armed with a machine pistol. At the back, with the tailboard lowered, sat the others, both armed with machine guns.

Len kept quite still, realising that from their position of superior height the Germans might see the Resistance group. The situation was dangerous. He was shocked when he heard Dievart say, 'When I give the order, fire!'

'God almighty, no!' Len said urgently. 'Everybody keep your heads right down out of sight! Don't fire, don't even move, it's our only hope.'

Dievart was furious. 'I am their leader and I give the orders!' He spoke so loudly that Len winced in anticipation of a fusillade from the cart. 'Who the hell do you think you are, Leonard!'

'You are completely mad!' Len whispered fiercely. 'Just keep out of sight until they are past and we can sort this out.'

Fortunately, the other two men saw the lunacy of attacking machine guns with one revolver, which was way out of range, and a mutilated shotgun. When the Germans had disappeared Len told the much older Dievart what he thought of his leadership. 'You aren't equipped to fight a running battle,' he said, 'and you can't fight machine guns with shotguns. All we can do is attack single soldiers and even then it's a gamble.' Dievart was unconvinced; he had been robbed of his moment of glory.

'I saved your life, you silly bugger,' Len said without anger and, replacing his rifle in the potato sack, he returned to Annoeullin to see if he could find a suitable war with a fifty-fifty chance of survival.

14

'MY GOD, IT'S LEONARD!'

On the outskirts of Annoeullin Len encountered a strange sight – armed German troops lining one side of the road were confronted by armed Resistance men on the other side. Despite the tension and danger women stood chatting on their doorsteps and one, stout, buxom and motherly, told Len that the Resistance men were demanding the surrender of all the German troops from the train.

The local schoolmaster, showing great courage and seeking to avoid bloodshed, approached the train commandant and suggested surrender. The commandant said that he would surrender to the first British officer to arrive but nothing would induce him to submit to civilians. He had the advantage, with about a thousand soldiers against fifty Resistance men, but the Frenchmen looked vengeful and full of hate and the officer was fearful. Len, watching, realised that one trigger-happy man on either side could precipitate a slaughter.

He collected Joseph Wiplier and they hurried to where René Saublin was directing another confrontation half a mile away. Here thirty Resistance men, well armed and in the protection of ditches were facing another strong group of Germans, who were decidedly more aggressive than their comrades at the station.

Marcel Fertein had hurried out from Lille and with René Saublin proposed to stop the two German groups from joining up. Len reported the explosive situation near the station and the ebullient René laughed. 'Well, if they want to surrender to a British officer we must supply them with one.'

'Just where will you find a British officer?' Len asked wrily.

René poked a finger in Len's chest. 'Here he is, right here!'

'I'm not an officer!' Len protested. 'I'm only a bloomin' private!'

'From this moment the Resistance promotes you captain,' René said. 'And come with me, I know where there is a complete British captain's uniform.' He had stolen it from British Army stores early in the war.

He brought out his Citroen car and with Len and an armed guard aboard, raced for the centre of Annoeullin but in the Grand Place two Resistance scouts stopped them and warned that fighting had broken out around the station. A Resistance man had fired at a German officer and missed him but the bullet had killed a woman looking from her window. The Germans, always quick to retaliate, were now firing at anybody on the streets.

René was disappointed as he turned his car around. 'Ah, well, Leonard, it was a good idea to promote you to captain and disarm them without a fight. Now it is too late. But consider yourself still a captain.' He went back to his own responsibilities while Len returned to join Joseph and together they watched the railway line, anticipating that the German soldiers would run along it. Before long they did just that and as the field-grey figures appeared Len gave a whoop of delight. 'Right, Joseph!' he said. 'This is where we start our war. Into that ditch!'

From cover, Len took careful aim at a German with his cavalry carbine and fired – and the recoil smashed against his shoulder. A second shot brought another painful hammer blow but Len thought he had nailed his man. As he stood to get a better view a hail of bullets spattered about him. Joseph was also having difficulty. He had fired one shot from his long carbine and now the breech was jammed. Cursing and swearing and almost sobbing he banged the weapon on the road, trying to free it. Len forced him to take cover. Len fired one more shot and cried out in pain as the butt once more slammed against his bruised shoulder. If all French weapons were of this standard he was not surprised that the French had been losing their wars.

By now the 200 Germans left on the train had surrendered to

four gendarmes and, disarmed, they were marched in the direction of Carvin to meet the advancing British Second Army. Len, anxious for more combat, also headed for Carvin where he and Jean-Baptiste Dievart – who was still affronted about being superseded in command of his Resistance group – observed two small Allied tanks racing towards Annoeullin. Some minutes later they saw the tricolour of France slowly fluttering to the top of the flagpole on the distant town hall of Annoeullin.

The people of Carvin, flocking into the streets, embraced one another and shouted, 'This is liberation! We are free! The English are here!'

Len mounted his bike for the umpteenth time that day and raced into Annoeullin to find flags and bunting and an atmosphere reminiscent of the euphoria of a pre-war Bastille Day. The festivity was premature, as Len found when one of René Saublin's men, driving a small van, screeched to a stop next to him. 'Shove your bike in the back, get in and cover my rear!' he yelled.

'What's happening?' Len shouted back.

'The Germans have returned in force from Sainghin and have advanced as far as the sawmills. René wants us to go round the town and warn everybody to get their flags out of sight in case the Germans take the town again.'

'Where have the British tanks gone?' Len asked.

'Back through Gondecourt towards Seclin.'

The driver and Len careered around Annoeullin shouting to the townspeople, 'The Germans are coming back! Flags down! Women and children to the cellars!'

Meanwhile, René Saublin and Marcel Fertein had had a narrow escape. Their men had held the Germans in a line of houses and René, with Marcel, had rushed to his house to get a fresh supply of British hand grenades. As they packed the bombs in packs, Marcel grabbed René's arm and hissed urgently. 'Don't move!' He indicated about twenty Germans in René's garden, crouching behind bushes. These men were outflanking the Resistance men while their comrades held them at the front. Alone except for a frightened young girl who helped René in his dental laboratory, the two men held grenades, withdrew the pins and waited on either side of the kitchen door. The Germans advanced cautiously, stopped unaccountably and chose to enter the house next door, which was empty. René and Marcel drew deep breaths as they replaced the grenade pins. After collecting half a dozen men to fire at this group of Germans, René sought out Len.

'Leonard, we must have those British tanks back here! Chase them in the van and tell them what is going on here.'

By now the van had a small tricolour fluttering from the radiator and Len, with the same driver, took the Gondecourt road, feeling that he was now playing a real part in the fighting war rather than the clandestine one he had known for so many years. In Gondecourt allied flags flew at every window and excited people were on the streets. Outside Buisine's garage stood a captured five-ton German Army truck flying a large tricolour and near Lesage Farm Len's little van nearly collided with one of the tanks coming from the other direction. They were the first British tanks to make contact with the enemy and their mission was extremely dangerous. The tank commander, a sergeant, leaned from the turret and shouted, 'Do you understand English?'

Len jumped from the van. 'Yes, what's happening?'

'Go no further along this road,' the sergeant said urgently. 'There's an enemy .88 anti-tank gun about five hundred yards to the left of the road and they got a direct hit on my other tank. We're armed only with a light mortar and a machine gun and we've radioed back for the heavies to help us.'

'What about the crew?' Len asked. 'Are they wounded?'

'I saw one man jump clear. They will be lying low until the heavies get here.' The sergeant waved and as the tank started off he called, 'Good luck!'

Len shouted back, 'By the way, I'm a British soldier from the BEF!'

The sergeant gave him a friendly grin. 'Yeah, and I'm a French soldier from Napoleon Bonaparte's army!'

Len explained the conversation to his driver and said,

disappointed, 'The tank commander doesn't believe that I'm British.'

'Who would?' the driver said. 'You look a typical Frenchman to us. You don't only talk our slang, you even have the accent of a coal miner!'

Len was both pleased and angry – pleased because at last here was a Frenchman telling him that he looked French, angry because his own compatriot did not recognise him as British. Driving forward as far as they dared, Len and the driver then approached on foot to see if they could help the crew of the knocked-out tank. They had covered half a mile when machine gun bullets hit the ground nearby and went ricocheting away with a whine. Diving into a ditch they saw the tank blazing furiously and, to their left, the threatening barrel of the dreaded German .88. German machine gunners were protecting the gun and, apparently fearing a British infantry attack, were sweeping the fields with bullets.

Returning by the van to Gondecourt, Len took his bike from the back and rode along the narrow track to Zelfa Ringot's house, where he exchanged news with Florentin Ringot before heading for the Dhenins' farm; he thought it might be worthwhile putting a couple of Resistance men there to keep watch on any German advance from that side. He left his rifle and his Resistance armband with Florentin and cycled off, suddenly aware that in this district everything was quiet, with neither cheering crowds nor flags.

Turning into the Wavrin road, he found himself facing a German half-track less than fifty yards away. Its heavy machine gun pointed straight at him and the gunner's finger was on the trigger. Four German storm troopers on motorbikes were also watching him. Had the Resistance emblem been on his arm or had the carbine been across his shoulder German bullets would have cut him in two. As it was, the situation was dangerous enough – he was the only civilian on the street and therefore a suspect Resistance man. Years of making quick decisions again came to Len's help. Hardly glancing at the Germans he casually leaned his bike against the wall of a house, opened the unlocked front door and walked in. Two strange women seated in the front room jumped up in fright but they knew him by sight and turned pale. One gasped, 'My God, it's Leonard!'

'Don't worry, girls, there's nothing to get alarmed about,' Len said, though he knew better. He pushed home the door bolt and glanced out the window. The four motorcyclists had walked their machines to the house and were looking curiously at Len's bike. As they beckoned the half-track forward Len prepared to slip out the back way – but the cyclists suddenly roared off into Gondecourt and the half-track followed.

Len quickly thanked the two unknown women, who were still speechless with fright, and followed the Germans into Gondecourt. They were racing along the Rue Nationale throwing grenades through the windows of every house that displayed allied flags. The Gondecourt Resistance had suffered casualties. The Germans had blown the bridge over the Houplin Canal and then placed machine guns in the houses facing the demolished bridge. This was standard military practice designed to catch enemy troops in the open as they tried to cross a waterway. The tactics did not usually trap well-trained soldiers but the Gondecourt Resistance men were not trained soldiers. They crossed the canal by the remaining shreds of bridge and as they reached the open space in front of the houses the German guns opened up. Five Gondecourt men were killed and others were wounded. Len had been telling his Resistance friends for years that they should never attack the Germans unless they knew they outnumbered them and then only if the enemy were in the open. As always, French impetuosity got in the way of common sense.

Once more back in Annouellin by van, Len found a big British command tank, with whose crew René Saublin and Marcel Fertein were vainly trying to communicate without a common language. Len became interpreter, passed on their tactical messages and then shook hands with the tank commander, a lieutenant. 'Are we pleased to see you!' he said.

'For a Frenchman you speak very good English,' the officer said.

'I *am* English,' Len practically shouted.

'Jolly good show, old chap. Might I ask what part of the services you belong to?'

'The Middlesex Regiment. I'm an escaped prisoner of war and I've been here since 1940.'

'Good God!' The officer was astounded. 'Do your people know that you are out here, alive and well?'

Len had sent some messages through to London to confirm his continued existence but he had no way of knowing if they had been received. He gave his regimental details to the tank officer who promised to radio them to London. On the officer's battle map Len marked where a German .88 anti-tank gun was camouflaged and other enemy positions. 'We'll deal with them,' the officer promised.

Marcel and René wanted local help from the British tanks but the officer on the spot was unable to provide it. His objective, as he explained through Len, was Antwerp and he could not stop to fight Germans on the way unless they forced him to fight. The Resistance would be achieving a great deal for the Allied offensive if they could hold the Germans in their present positions. This Marcel Fertein promised to do.

At this point there came into Len's Resistance life one of the most extraordinary characters he had ever met. He was riding a motorbike and he introduced himself as Jack Farnell and said he had 'become detached' from his unit. At first Len took him for a dashing and unconventional commando or special services officer, the type who would make single-handed attacks against a German headquarters, shoot the general, and, speaking faultless German, order the artillery to fire on their own armour. He had that kind of appearance, Jack Farnell. He wore a new type of American-style crash helmet and a well-cut, expensive trench coat that reached down to his highly polished boots. Two outside dispatch cases hung from the rear of his motorbike; as Len was to find out, they were stuffed with French currency. Actually only an officer's batman, Farnell was always conveniently getting himself lost in his search for more and more loot, and he had no intention of getting into a fight.

He followed the scouting light tanks and then, as the Resistance proudly brought out their German captives, Farnell calmly searched them for watches and money. The French always overlooked something. He had already acquired fifteeen watches, which he wore gauntlet-like on both arms.

On this first meeting, Len believed that Farnell really had lost his unit and warned him that groups of Germans were in every direction. 'It's all right if I stick to you, then?' Farnell asked, when he learned that Len was working with the Resistance.

Len could hardly have been more pleased. 'We'll do it the other way round,' he said. 'I'll stick to you on the pillion seat.'

It was the first time he had ridden pillion and after all the hard pedalling he had done on a pushbike the experience was exhilarating. As they arrived at the Annoeullin level crossing twelve huge Sherman tanks, with British crews, rumbled out of the Carvin road. They were the spearhead of a tremendous armoured column of self-propelled guns, half-tracks, more tanks, bridge-builders, Bren-carriers and supply vehicles. The British army was passing through in force. The French were by now hysterical with joy, rushing out to offer the British carefully hoarded champagne, beer, cognac and every kind of wine. Girls threw themselves on the road in front of the tanks so that the drivers had to stop; then they clambered aboard the juggernauts to embrace the crew. Tough tank commanders, garlanded with flowers, looked as if they were taking part in a mock beauty competition. The column took three hours to pass and by that time the people of Annoeullin had cheered themselves hoarse.

Walking through the excited crowd, Len heard Amelie Sion calling him, 'Voilà Leonard!' Rushing across the road to embrace him she cried to the crowd, 'He is an English soldier that has been with us since 1940! Vive l'armée anglaise! Vive Angleterre!'

The volatile crowds took up her cry and scores of people shook Len by the hand, embraced and kissed him, thumped him on the back and wept over him. An old lady said emotionally, 'My God, he is so young!'

Overwhelmed by the depth of their feeling but grateful for it and emotional himself, Len could only stammer, 'Merci, merci . . . vive la France!' He had become separated from Jack Farnell but now saw him and called out. The crowd, too, saw the British uniform and another wave of shouting ensued. 'Un soldat Anglais! Vive l'armée anglaise!'

As the pressure eased around Len, he ducked into a cafe for a quick beer and dropped a five-franc note on the bar. 'Nobody pays for drinks today,' the owner, a woman, said, pushing it back to him, 'least of all an Englishman.' She gave Len an embrace and kiss.

Outside in the sun Farnell was deliriously enjoying himself as the women queued up to embrace him and Len had to drag him away from them. 'Jesus, Len,' Farnell said, 'these women all want to get into bed with me! I can feel it!'

'You'd also feel six inches of knife,' Len said wrily, 'French men are very possessive.'

'But those hot women . . . !' Farnell said with heavy sighs. He threw kisses to the women he was being forced to leave. 'What's the hurry, Len?'

'It's time we caught up with the British column,' Len said impatiently.

Chasing the tanks on the motorbike, the two men soon found that six Shermans had detoured to deal with the .88 and one tank shell had penetrated the breechblock, splitting the barrel open banana-skin fashion. The mutilated crew lay dead around their gun. The armoured column, pushing on, had left a battery of field guns to protect its flanks and Len was intrigued and alarmed to note that the guns were pointed the wrong way, back towards Gondecourt.

Leaving Jack with the bike, he hurried to the guns and the captain who appeared to be in command. As he proposed to give the gunner captain some advice he decided to keep to his Resistance identity and to maintain his recent promotion to captain, just to even things up a bit. He reckoned that to introduce himself as a private of infantry and proffer advice on artillery tactics might not go down too well.

The gunner, seeing Len's approach, said courteously, and with an Oxford accent, 'Bonjour, m'sieur.'

'Bonjour, mon capitaine,' Len said. 'Allow me to introduce myself – Capitaine Manessier, French Resistance.'

'How do you do,' the gunner said. 'I'm always pleased to meet anybody who speaks good English.' He offered his hand.

Len pointed towards Gondecourt. 'Why are your guns pointing in that direction? It is wrong. The enemy are behind you, in the forts of Houplins and Noyelles. They're only a mile away. If the Germans attack, that is where they will come from.'

'That may be so,' the captain said unworried, 'but I have my instructions and I am in position as ordered. There must be a good reason for such orders.'

Len had heard all this before and knew that orders always overrode common sense. 'I assure you, though,' he said, 'the danger comes from your rear.'

'What worries me most,' the captain said, 'is that I have no infantry to protect my guns. Should we be attacked we are in an exposed position. Shots were fired from that wood just fifteen minutes ago.'

Len knew the woods, Bois de Loup, and offered to try to raise enough Resistance men to comb the place and flush out any Germans. But his more immediate problem was to mediate between Jack Farnell and a heavily armed, very elderly French civilian. On him Len counted five rifles, two light machine guns and four pistols, all German. He was bowed under the weight. Jack, an inveterate scrounger, wanted the superb Luger the old man had in his belt.

'What do you want with all those weapons?' Len asked the white-haired warrior.

'I'm a fighting man,' he growled, 'but our local Resistance leader told me that I'm too old to join his group. Too old be damned! I'm showing him whether I'm too old. I walked over to the German lines and shot three Boche with this.' He indicated a World War I revolver. 'Then I gathered all the firearms that were lying around. When I've shown them to my leader you can have the lot.'

'O.K., old man,' Len said. 'You show them to your chief, then bring them back. We can make good use of them. While you are with your chief give him a message from the English captain.'

'What does he want?'

'He needs all the men your chief can spare, right here, to protect his guns from German attacks. Tell your chief to send men at once.'

'I'll tell him – and I'll be back to help you myself.' The old man swore violently. 'Call themselves Resistance leaders! They can't even recognise a good man when they see one.' He cocked a thumb at the British captain. 'Ça va?'

The gunner gave him the thumbs-up sign and the old man, weighed down with his weapons, stumbled down the road.

'Do you think he'll be all right?' Farnell asked anxiously.

'Don't worry about that old chap,' Len said. 'He's a fighter.'

'I'm not worried about him, just about my Luger,' Farnell said.

'Bugger your Luger,' Len said. 'Let's get into that wood.' He led the way towards the trees and then sprays of machine gun bullets sent him and Farnell flying into a small trench.

'Damn it!' Farnell said in a shrill voice. 'Those were bullets!'

'What did you expect in a battle?' Len asked him. 'Ping-pong balls?'

The trench was already occupied by two young Frenchmen armed with German rifles. They pointed out a ditched van, captured with its German occupants by two Resistance men but lost to machine gun fire from Noyelles fort. One German had been killed, another was wounded and the two Frenchmen were pinned down in a beet field.

Following the request for reinforcements, about a dozen Reistance men arrived in a rush. Most were teenagers and they were led by a young blond man red in the face and full of the courage that comes from too much wine. 'Forward my friends!' and the younger men began to follow him into the beet field.

'Stop!' Len yelled and jumped out of the trench to bar the way. 'You're heading for certain death that way!' The German machine gunners supported his point of view by firing at the group, who dived for the trench – all except the leader who returned to the edge of the trench and looked around him in an uncomprehending daze.

'Come on!' he shouted. 'I'm not afraid of a few Boche. Let's get after them.'

The youths, rather troubled, looked at Len, who said, 'If he wants to commit suicide, that's his business.'

'But we will have no leader,' one boy said.

'You're better off with no leader than a drunken one,' Len advised him.

A long burst of machine gun fire brought the blond leader into the discussion. 'You know,' he said to Len, waving his rifle dangerously, 'I would be within my rights to shoot that lot for refusing to obey an order.'

Len began to act like Capitaine Manessier again. 'If you make threats of that sort we will disarm you. You are more of a danger to us than the Germans. Go back to town, sleep off the drink, and come back when you're sober.'

'I'll be back,' the blond said sourly. 'Then we'll see who gives the orders.'

As he headed out of the firing line, a spokesman for the others said, 'Can we join up with you?' He gave Len a rough salute. 'The truth is, we haven't the faintest idea what to do.'

'Right,' said Len, 'you've signed up.' He explained the needs of the British artillery commander. 'We're going to check out the woods and then clear them of Germans. After that we will take up positions to stop the Germans attacking from Houplins.' Having informed the gunners of his intentions, Len split the Resistance boys into two groups. 'Here, Jack,' he said with all the authority of 'Capitaine Manessier', 'You take this patrol through the wood on the right side and I'll take my patrol on the other side.'

Farnell stared at him in utter astonishment. 'You want me to lead a patrol?'

'You're the only other trained soldier here,' Len said. 'These boys don't know infantry tactics.'

'Infantry tactics be damned!' Farnell said. 'I'm an officer's batman!'

'Then you've got a bloomin' big advantage,' Len said. 'How many times have you heard his nibs talking about tactics? Get moving.'

Farnell moved off reluctantly and the young Resistance men, who had understood nothing of the conversation, went with him eagerly. They were convinced from his appearance that a British hero was leading them into battle.

Advancing through the trees, Len became the veteran infantryman again, moving his men in open order and using the trees as cover. He found a German bunker and, ordering his Resistance boys to cover him, he crawled forward until he could fire a shot into it. When there was no response he entered to find many signs that it had been recently abandoned. Towards the other side of the woods they came to a house and a frightened couple, aged about fifty, appeared at the door.

'Seen any Germans around here?' Len said.

'We haven't seen anybody all day,' the man replied.

Len was mildly puzzled by the couple's fear but he put this down to the roar of battle which had been going on for hours, and carried on with his fighting patrol. He had made a mistake and should have searched the house; three Germans had the couple covered with their revolvers. British infantry took them prisoner the next day.

At the fringe of the wood Len positioned his men to watch the town of Houplins in the distance. Two British Shermans appeared from the direction of Gondecourt, ignored heavy machine gun fire from Noyelles fort, and stopped about 500 yards from two large haystacks. Their guns swivelled, aimed and let fly with a roar – and the haystacks disintegrated. About thirty Germans who had been concealed there burst forth, scuttling like so many ants from a disturbed nest, only to be met by machine gun fire from the tanks. It was a deadly and efficient action. Other tanks and motorised infantry arrived with the news that the Germans had pulled out of Houplins and Len then considered himself relieved of his Resistance command.

'Capitaine Manessier' shook hands with the gunner captain and called Jack from his patrol. As far as Len could see Farnell had made no progress at all on his side of the wood, and the batman was thankful to bid farewell to the Resistance boys; they were too eager to find trouble.

'That old man hasn't come back with the Luger,' he complained.

'He probably needs it more than you do,' Len said with a sarcasm that was lost on Farnell. 'Forget it and let's catch up with the war.'

15

TWO-MAN TASK FORCE

Farnell retrieved his motor bike from its hiding place and with Len on the pillion behind him rode into the centre of Seclin. Here they saw a British army chaplain standing beside his Austin Seven and Jack braked to a sliding stop next to him. The chaplain was angry and upset about a German massacre in the town and he tapped the butt of a revolver tucked into the open front of his battle jacket. 'I only hope that I come up against a few of the bloody bastards,' he said. 'I'll make them pay with this.'

Len, surprised by the chaplain's language, but applauding his healthy hatred of Germans, introduced himself in his own name – Len Arlington of the Middlesex Regiment, escaper and Resistance fighter.

'In that case I've got something for you,' the chaplain said. Rummaging among boxes on the back seat of the Austin he produced five packets of twenty Players cigarettes. 'These are for distribution among British troops,' he said, 'and you qualify.'

He waved cheerfully as he drove off, hoping to commit murder against German butchers.

Jack and Len wondered about their next part in the war when a Frenchman wearing beret and overalls came out of a warehouse and said ingratiatingly to Jack, 'Does the British officer need anything in the way of drinks and tobacco?' As Len had done, he assumed that Jack was an officer.

Jack did nothing to disabuse him of the idea and he was indeed interested in drinks and tobacco and everything else he could lay his hands on. He and Len followed the stranger into a nearby large warehouse where the Germans had stored goods looted from the French. From here it had been shipped back to Germany. That morning Len saw great stacks of cases of champagne, wine, cigarettes and tobacco. The two British soldiers helped themselves to a few packets of cigarettes and cigars and accepted a glass of champagne from the Frenchman. But it was hardly a happy occasion, for this man was to give them the first full account of what had happened in Seclin on the previous day, Friday. It had all begun there, in the warehouse.

A group of Resistance men had captured the two Germans left to guard the building. When they saw that it was a type of robbers' Aladdin's Cave, they had the bright idea of enticing other Germans inside, and then taking them prisoner. One Resistance man stood outside the gates with a bottle of champagne hidden close by; when a solitary German appeared, or even two enemy, he offered them a drink. There was plenty more inside, he said, and they could help themselves. At first suspicious and on the alert for ambush, the Germans were gradually lulled into a state bordering on the euphoric, first by the sight of the luxuries and then by taste and smell. Once they had relaxed enough to lean their weapons against a crate while they sampled the good things being offered, the hidden Resistance men pounced. By noon the group had taken eleven prisoners without harming any of them. The Resistance men, cheerfully imbibing free champagne, were soon careless; they even forgot that Seclin was still in German hands. The leader had ordered his men not to show themselves on the streets with their weapons but one man wandered out into the Rue de Houplins to stare at a flight of Spitfires – and he carried his rifle over his shoulder.

He neither saw nor heard, until too late, a German motor-bike combination as it turned into the road, but the SS officer in the passenger seat saw him. Drawing his revolver, he shouted 'Terrorist!' and opened fire.

The Resistance man raced for the gates and from shelter fired three quick, useless shots at the fast disappearing bike. After a conference, the Resistance group decided that, with the area changing hands, the incident could be ignored. But the SS officer, wanting revenge, collected in Houplins a company of SS men, and rushed them in trucks back to Seclin.

Firing from the hip, they stormed into the warehouse and mowed down the Resistance men; those who were only wounded were finished off with a pistol bullet through the head. The group then moved threateningly through Seclin, taking prisoner every man they could find, about thirty of them. As they were marched along the Rue d'Arras towards the outskirts of Seclin, a woman of thirty saw her brother among the prisoners and rushing into the middle of the road she dropped to her knees and begged the SS officer to spare the men. He laughed and merely told four men to bring the women with the men, and she was dragged along. Marched into a large field near the Quinquette Cafe they were lined up with their backs to a pit about fifty feet in length, five feet across and six deep; it was normally used to make beet compost.

Six Germans formed the firing squad and all fired individual bursts at each Frenchman in turn. Every man knew therefore when his turn had come. A seventeen-year-old boy said to his neighbour, a middle-aged man, 'I think I'm going to faint.' The man said, 'Give me your hand and give your other hand to the man on your right. Don't be afraid. Show these German scum how Frenchmen can die.'

The bursts of bullets came closer and the boy trembled. 'Courage, lad,' the man said. 'Close your eyes and pray.'

As the German bullets killed the older man he fell backwards and dragged the boy with him; he knew he had been hit in the shoulder but was soon unconscious. As the last man fell the excited and laughing Germans kicked into the pit the two or three bodies which had fallen on the edge. Two soldiers jumped in to shoot through the head any victim who might have survived. Bales of straw were then thrown on top of the corpses.

The woman had fainted from sheer horror and terror but as she recovered the SS men stripped her and raped her in turn. Then she was turned face down, shot through the back of the head and thrown into the pit. The straw was set alight.

Covered with blood and weighed down by corpses the boy recovered consciousness. He was in danger of being suffocated by the smoke from the damp hay but hearing the Germans talking he dared not move. Hours later, he dragged himself painfully from under the bodies of the other men of Seclin and crawled to a nearby house.

Late in the evening the deeply distressed and angry townspeople took the bodies to the concert hall, where many hundreds of people congregated to mourn the tragedy. All this had taken place only a few hundred feet from where Len Arlington and Jack Farnell sat drinking champagne and among the crates around them several Resistance men had perished. Suddenly there seemed to be no sparkle in the champagne. 'By God,' Len said, 'if we take any SS men prisoner they'll get no quarter.'

The British liberation swept on and by next morning the German army no longer controlled Seclin and Resistance men managed to trap an officer and a sergeant who had taken part in the massacre. Len and Jack Farnell had stayed in Seclin and Len was with the Resistance group, led by a Pole, when they marched the two Germans into the concert hall to view the bodies. 'Take a good look at the work of the glorious German Army,' the Pole ordered them.

The Germans hung back but rifle muzzles jabbed them forward. The leader kicked the officer in the back, sending him sprawling. 'Advance and salute the corpses!' he shouted.

Getting to his feet the officer snapped to attention and raised his right arm in the Nazi salute. 'Heil Hitler!' he cried.

The Pole punched him violently on the nose and as blood gushed, he turned to the sergeant. 'How about you? Do you feel like giving the Nazi salute?'

'Nein, nein, moi camarade!' the German whined.

When they had been pushed and dragged outside the town hall the officer turned to the Resistance chief and said with great formality, 'I am a prisoner of war. I demand that you hand me and my sergeant over to the British military authorities.'

The Resistance leader was already angry; this request, made as if the German officer considered himself above punishment for his appalling crime, drove him to fury. 'Leonard,' he said, 'what do we do with these bastards?'

Len didn't hesitate. 'You'd better shoot them before the British get here,' he said. 'They're too soft.'

The Pole shot both men dead with his revolver. The people of Seclin, deep in shock over the massacre of their friends and relations, were silent; a quick killing was too good for such criminals. Most of them wished they could get their hands on more Germans.

Len and Jack set off once more to chase the armoured column, this time to Lille. A Resistance man had told them that the Resistance had taken prisoner most of the Lille garrison but fighting was still going on. By now the Resistance was openly organising and at the town of Roncin a long queue of men were lining up to seek ammunition for scores of different weapons. They all wanted to go and kill Germans, and the Resistance ordnance section could provide most of them with the calibre of rounds they sought. Len was able to get cartridges for his cavalry carbine, which he tried out in the street. The loud report so alarmed the town that war nearly broke out again as men dived for cover.

After yet another drink with a woman overjoyed at meeting a British officer – Jack Farnell – and a genuine Resistance man, Len, they headed for Lille where they rode in triumph down the Rue de Faubourg and Rue Solferino. Arriving at the Place du Theatre, Jack drew up at the Cafe du Cocq Hardi, took off his enormous coat and in battledress he made for the door, accompanied by Len. And that was how, that Saturday morning, they became the first British soldiers to enter the great city of Lille. The advancing armoured column had bypassed it. Privates Farnell and Arlington received, on behalf of the British Army, the cheers and gratitude of the populace.

'Un Anglais!' a man shouted when he saw Jack at the door of the cafe, 'C'est un Anglais. The English have arrived!'

As Jack was mobbed by a crowd of young people and hugged and hungrily kissed by the girls, Len, in civilian clothing, felt left out and was rather aggrieved. He tried to get Jack to leave, on the grounds that a riot might develop but

Jack was enjoying himself immensely. A girl gave him a bouquet, took his head in her hands and passionately kissed him on the lips.

The crowd went wild. 'Bravo! Vive les Anglais!'

'I don't know what they're talking about, Len,' Jack said breathlessly, 'but I like it. Let's go on liberating this place.'

An old man with a goatee beard exploded a champagne bottle's cork and handed the foaming bottle to Jack. 'Drink Englishman, to France and England!'

Len checked the batman with the bottle to his lips and whispered. 'Don't drink before you shout "France et Angleterre!" to the crowd.'

This toast went down so well that the crowd sang the English national anthem and then the *Marseillaise* and many sobbed with emotion. 'Lord, I could stay here for ever,' Jack said. 'I could get used to this.'

But Len eased him away from his new friends and he rode his bike in stately progress through Place de la République and Boulevarde de la Liberté with the general idea of heading for the Belgian frontier. The pair came across a large group of German soldiers, hands behind their heads, guarded by just four young Frenchmen. Jack began to go glassy eyed, which Len was beginning to recognise as a symptom of his compulsion for scrounging. Stopping his bike and walking into the middle of the road, he held up his hand commandingly.

'What the hell are you doing?' Len demanded.

'I just want to question a few of these bastards,' Jack said.

Len explained to the young Resistance men that the British captain wanted to interrogate a few prisoners but they were uneasy. 'We cannot stop the prisoners here!' the leader said. 'With sixty of them and only four of us they could overpower us. If the officer wants to question prisoners, tell him to go to the citadelle. We've got plenty there!'

Len guided Jack to the old barracks where they were passed through to a senior officer of the Resistance dressed in a beautiful uniform, riding breeches and boots. 'Bonjour, commandant,' Len said. 'I am Captain Arlington of the British

Army and also Capitaine Manessier of the Resistance and this is Captain Farnell. He wishes to question some prisoners.'

'Of course,' the officer said and had some Germans brought into the courtyard. 'You are the first British officers to arrive, Intelligence, of course?'

'Of course,' Len said.

'Your troops are on the way, no doubt?' the officer asked hopefully.

'A strong detachment is rushing to take over the town's defence,' Len assured him.

'Before the Germans left the citadelle they slit the throats of fifteen Russian prisoners of war,' the Resistance man said. 'Would you like to view the corpses?'

Len was not enthusiastic and Jack, when the offer was put to him, was horrified. It was unusual for the Germans to cut throats, Len knew, they usually hanged or shot their victims. About a hundred prisoners were paraded for the British officer, a German-speaking French guard stood by and Len acted as British official interpreter. 'O.K. Jack,' he said. 'Fire away with your questions.'

He supposed that Jack must have learned something about interrogation from the officer for whom he was batman and he was interested to observe his technique.

Jack marched along the rows of prisoners, eyed them ferociously, then stopped and shouted. 'Do any of you speak English?'

After a short silence, a hesitant voice said, 'Yes, sir, I do.'

Jack fixed this German with a sneer. 'So, you speak good English?'

'I worked in England before the war.'

Jack put his face close to the prisoner and barked, 'As what? A fifth columnist?' He laughed cynically. 'I want you to tell your mates that we, the British, think that you are all a shower of filthy bastards.'

Len looked at the ceiling and hoped that the senior French Resistance officer's English was inadequate to understand Jack's comment. When the German looked confused, Jack swore at him. 'Well,' he said, 'what are you waiting for? Tell them what we think of all you German bastards.'

Len coughed. 'I think he could be having trouble understanding some of your words.'

'I'll give him trouble!' Jack snarled. But by now the German had managed to find a translation, which he passed on to the sullen ranks.

Jack was eyeing a watch-chain fastened to a button of the German's tunic and now he grabbed it. A sharp tug produced a large onion-shaped watch on the end of the chain. 'You know very well that prisoners of war are not allowed to keep watches,' he said fiercely. 'Take it off!'

The German, on the verge of tears said, 'It was a present from my dead father and has great sentimental value; please let me keep it!'

The supervising French officer asked Len what all the fuss was about and Len said urgently, 'For God's sake Jack. You are a British officer, remember? A captain, British officers do not go around grabbing prisoners' watches.'

But Captain Jack had a crazy acquisitive gleam in his eye and Len was worried that he might order the entire parade to turn out their pockets. 'Give the poor bastard back his watch,' he said, and Farnell reluctantly did so.

Len took control of the situation and told the French officer that as the British captain had finished with the prisoners they could be returned to their cells. He kept the French officer talking and moved away with him so that he would not see Jack fossicking amid a heap of soldiers' rubbish – old razors, shaving brushes, cakes of soap, odd cartridge cases, the hundreds of items which soldiers acquire. As they returned to the bike, accompanied by a fifteen-year-old Resistance fighter who was acclaimed by his comrades for having already killed two SS men, Jack pushed into Len's hand a small, black round object. It was a German grenade – and Len was startled to discover that the safety pin had been removed and that he was holding down the striker lever. 'Hang on to it,' Jack said urgently. 'I took out the pin and can't get it back in.'

Len swore at him and carefully handed the bomb to the Resistance boy, who took it off to throw in the canal.

Crossing the Belgian frontier, the Special Force of Private Farnell and Private Arlington reached Tournai, where the British Army was much in evidence. The sign 'Town Major' attracted Len and he walked in on a young lieutenant who, in very good French, said, 'Good day, sir, what can I do for you?'

'I'm an escaped British prisoner of war,' Len said. 'I've been fighting with the French Resistance and I need some identity papers. All I have right now are forged French Resistance identity cards.'

'Forged!' the young officer said. 'Good Lord!'

'To fool the Nazis,' Len explained patiently.

'Oh, I see. I can give you a chit stating who you are. It will give you authority to move around the British area.'

'And how do I go about getting back to England?'

He was advised to make his own way to Paris where there was a repatriation unit at Hotel George V to look after escaped prisoners of war. To get there, said the lieutenant, he could provide an authority for Len to commandeer any civilian vehicle. He asked if Len had had any experience of German booby traps. Very many civilians had been killed or wounded at Berque, near Dunkirk, where the Germans had planted landmines in a baker's shop. They left a loaf of bread in full view in the window and when it was moved by a hungry looter the mines exploded. Len told him about the German massacres in his area of France.

He returned to the street to find Jack Farnell trying to commandeer a small van from its owner, a small dark Belgian aged about forty-five, wearing blue overalls. He was explaining to Jack, who did not understand a word, that the vehicle had been hidden from the Germans since 1940 and would need an overhaul. Jack had collected too much loot to be carried on a motorbike and was hell-bent on acquiring a car or van. He flagged down a passing British 15-cwt truck, attached the van to it with a tow rope and spent a fruitless hour dragging it around Tournai trying to get it started. Len, who knew these people better than Jack did, suspected that the owner had removed the rotor arm. He also suspected that it was time he parted from Jack before they were both arrested for posing as officers or some other crime. He left Jack already planning his next scrounging coup.

16

'YOU TOOK YOUR TIME COMING BACK'

Half an hour later, at a major crossroads in Tournai, Len encountered a British major and two captains directing traffic. They glanced at Len with a carbine over his shoulder and wearing a tricolour armband and the major said, 'Good day, sir. You must be French.'

'You're wrong there,' Len said. 'I'm a British escaped prisoner of war and I have been fighting with the French Resistance.'

'And from what regiment?'

'The Middlesex.' He omitted mention of rank, knowing from experience that conversation dried up when people learned that he was a private.

'I say, did you hear that, you fellows?' the major exclaimed. 'This chap is an escaped prisoner of war, he's British and he's been fighting with the French Resistance.'

'Good show!' the captains said, without much interest.

'When were you captured?' the major asked.

'Dunkirk, 1940.'

'And how long have you been on the run?'

'Since June 1940.'

'Good God!' the major exclaimed. 'Do you mean to say that you have been hiding in German-occupied territory for going on five years? That's bloody amazing.'

It's bloody miraculous, Len told himself. At that moment a German staff car, a grand Mercedes, approached the crossroads. But it did not carry Germans. In the front seat were two British soldiers and in the back, alone, was a short, slight man with a hooked nose, and he was wearing a black beret.

The major hissed, 'It's General Montgomery!' He and the captains jumped into line and stood rigidly to attention. As the car slowly passed them the major, in the right, saluted. Monty lifted a hand in acknowledgement and gave Len an amused glance. Len returned the compliment with a bold wink and the thumbs-up. 'Hello, me old cock,' he said loudly. 'You took your bloody time coming back.' And the car went on.

The captains were not amused but the major laughed. 'Come on,' he said, 'I must buy you a drink and hear something about your time in France.'

But friendly though he was, he could not provide transport going south in France. After a lightning northwards dash of 362 kilometres in four days, on September 3 the British Army had liberated Brussels, on the following day they had captured Antwerp and now everything on wheels was heading further north for the push against the Germans in Holland.

As Len waited impatiently for a lift at the Tournai crossroads a tall, very thin Belgian approached and asked him if he was a member of the 'White Army', a major Belgian resistance group. Len said he did not have that honour but that he was a member of the French Resistance.

'Ah,' the tall man said with satisfaction, 'would you like to capture an SS swine who is hiding in a house near here?'

After the massacres at Ascq and Seclin – he had not yet heard about the many other massacres – Len would like nothing better than to catch an SS man. Needing help, he visited the British Military Police post nearby and without telling the captain in command that he was British, asked for the loan of a couple of soldiers to capture the SS man. He was persuasive and the captain lent him a sergeant major and four men and told them to take orders from Len.

The Belgian led them to a house where the wanted man was supposed to be and Len led a surprise attack; he knew from his experience at the hands of the Germans that these tactics worked. They found no SS man in the house but Len was suspicious of the housewife's manner and kept the MPs with him. The Belgian informer came running to say that the SS man had now been sighted in the railway station cafe. Len used the same tactics – two MPs went straight through the cafe to the back garden, two stayed at the front door and Len and the sergeant major entered.

To their surprise, the large place was full of British troops drinking, with their Sten guns and rifles piled high on a table. On Len's request, the CSM ordered all the British to pick up their weapons and leave. Len asked the proprietor if she knew personally all thirty civilians remaining and she admitted that some were strangers. Len began to examine identity cards while the soldier covered him. After dealing with half the people present he noticed a man of about twenty-five with a girl by his side – and she was terrified. Puzzled, Len looked around and saw that the Belgian informer was frantically pointing a finger at the young man. 'That's him!' he cried.

Len poked his carbine into the man's stomach, 'Put your hands in the air.'

Startled by this sudden action, the sergeant major leapt to cover the suspect, his Sten gun only inches from his face. The girl screamed. Motioning the sergeant major back, Len frisked the man but he carried no weapons. He was sorry for the girl and said, 'There is no need for alarm, mademoiselle, we are not Gestapo thugs.'

The man handed Len a Belgian identity card, issued at the town hall and dated 1939.

'As a Belgian national you should surely have renéwed this card,' Len said.

'Yes, but I have lost it,' he said sullenly.

Len turned to the girl. 'Do you kow this man?'

'Yes,' she said quietly, 'he's my fiancé.'

Len was still suspicious. 'Have you ever served in the German Army?' he asked the man sharply.

When the man was silent the Belgian informer rushed up and punched him on the face, screaming abuse. 'Tell everybody how long you served in the Waffen SS! I suppose you will now say that you were forced to join.'

Len asked the sergeant major to turn out the suspect's

pockets and when that was done, Len himself examined each item in turn. He found what he was looking for – a German Army paybook, made out in this man's name and giving the date of his enlistment as April 1942.

Len gave him a long, hard look. 'I suppose you know what this means?'

'I soon realised the mistake I had made in joining the Germans and I deserted,' the young man said with a mixture of desperation and pleading.

Len was angry now; he knew the brutal reputation of the Waffen SS. 'Oh yes!' he said bitterly. 'You deserted once you realised that Germany had lost the war.' He examined the paybook again. 'You served on the Russian front. You are no longer a Belgian national – you gave up that nationality when you enlisted in 1942. You are bloody lucky you are not in France. The Resistance would shoot you on the spot as a traitor.'

They marched the man and the weeping girl to the Military Police post to await the arrival of Belgian police. The case of treason against him was so conclusive that he would have little chance of escaping a firing squad. The captain, pleased by the success of the little operation, offered Len the use of an American jeep and the sergeant major as driver to return to France. And that was how he arrived back in Chemy, the Faucomprez family and a flurry of embraces and kisses. Pleased though he was to be home, Len was acutely aware that the Germans were still in strength less than twenty miles away and he slept with his rifle under his hand on the bed.

Anxious to get his position clarified, he returned to Lille next day to locate the Town Major and report back to the Army. A friendly military policeman showed him the way and late that morning he found himself sitting in front of the major, explaining who he was and asking for instructions.

The major pushed him a slip of paper and a pen and said, 'Would you write down your name, rank and number, also your regiment, where you were taken prisoner, where you escaped and the names of all the people who helped you. Then, briefly, describe what has happened to you since you escaped.'

The form measured six inches by four inches. Len laughed. He couldn't help laughing. And he cried. He couldn't help crying. 'I'm sorry, sir,' he said at last. 'I think I need something bigger than this.'

He got something bigger – two exercise books – and was given three days to write his account. Back at Chemy he returned his borrowed rifle and was busy and happy and, for the first time, relaxed. Old friends cycled from Annoeullin to wish him good luck . . . the entire Wiplier family of Joseph, Lucienne, Henri, Jo-Jo and Lucette. Formally, he asked Pierre and Fi-Fi for their permission to marry Marcelle, now eighteen, and received it.

But he was now once more under Army orders and in Lille he was sent to join another twenty Allied servicemen, mostly air crew who had been shot down and had then evaded the Germans, and a few recent soldier escapers. Len became friendly with a fair-haired Canadian in his thirties, wearing grey flannel trousers and a sports jacket. On their way to Paris and the repatriation unit, they picked up an American tail-gunner who had bailed out of a Flying Fortress by mistake. Thinking his plane was doomed after a mid-air collision, he had jumped but as he floated down he saw it continuing steadily on. 'Sure as hell they'll courtmartial me,' he told the escapers. 'Well, who'd like to share my emergency rations? This is sure as hell an emergency!' Len had another laugh – the flier's emergency rations contained some toilet paper. The people of occupied France had not seen such a thing in years.

At Hotel George V Len's friend, the Canadian, signed the register as requested and handed the pen to Len. 'O.K. chum, it's all yours.'

Len wrote: 'Private Leonard Arlington 6203445. Middlesex Regiment,' and glanced casually at the Canadian's entry: 'John Applestone, Wing Commander, Royal Canadian Air Force.' He had supposed that this quiet little man was of lowly rank, instead he was equivalent to a lieutenant colonel in the British Army – a battalion commander. Len was tremendously impressed by his modesty. The group was astonished, though delighted, to find that each man had been allotted a private

suite complete with bathroom. As Len stood in the middle of
the big bedroom, almost alarmed by a standard of luxury he
had never seen before – except briefly in the chateau when on
the run in 1940 – the wing commander walked in. 'I've got the
room next door,' he said. Walking around Len's room he said
appreciatively, 'It's not bad, eh? Up to Savoy standards.'

Private Arlington was tongue-tied; now that he knew this
man's rank he was uncertain how to address him.

'What's the matter?' Applestone asked. 'You look kind of
funny.'

'I'm sorry,' Len said, 'but I noticed your rank in the register.
You should have told me you are a wing commander.' He was
mildly reproachful.

'What the hell for?' Applestone said, puzzled.

'Have you any idea what my rank is? It's the lowest in the
British Army. I'm not even an NCO.'

Applestone put his hand on Len's shoulder. 'Look chum,' he
said. 'In the Canadian forces we don't pull rank. We are all
fighting the same war together. Take yourself – you proved
yourself just as worthy as any top ranking general. Forget about
rank and when you're ready we'll go out together and see
something of the night life of Paris.'

They were all issued with American uniforms – the only ones
available – and that afternoon they saw General de Gaulle making
a triumphant progress on foot down the Champs Elysées, during
which French traitors who had helped the Gestapo tried to snipe
him. The tall de Gaulle did not deign to stoop.

Len spent just one night in Hotel George V; next day a truck
took the British to the Hotel Maurice, where, British Army
fashion, officers were separated from other ranks; the men were
sent to a transit camp, the officers to the Commodore Hotel.
The men's next meal was served straight from the cookhouse
into their newly issued mess tins.

As part of his security check Len was interviewed by no less
an Intelligence celebrity than Colonel Maurice Buckmaster, a
man the Nazis hated. It was Buckmaster who sent Michael
Trotobas to France and who had masterminded so many of the

SOE's operations in France. Len had a lot to say about 'Captain Jack Evans', 'Joe' and Alex Keiller, among others, and Buckmaster was so impressed that he sent the young soldier on to Military Intelligence (MI5) in Whitehall.

Here Len met two young men in mufti who asked him a lot of questions but he soon had the dreadful feeling that he was not getting his story across to them. To be fair to them, Len was having difficulties with his language; it was a mixture of English and northern French patois. No doubt his adventures did seem a little improbable and finally one of the young men asked, 'Have you left a girlfriend back there in France?'

Len saw the drift of the question at once. They thought he was making up a story as a reason for getting to France again.

These young men, who perhaps were doing valuable war work, had seen no *active* service. Len Arlington was too modest to tell them all that he had experienced, just as he had written his report in the exercise books in a routine, undramatic way. But his achievement should be stressed. While the war lasted he had seen, probably, more armed German soldiers than any other British soldier who had remained free. Nobody could have remained longer at large, with the Germans hunting him, than Len Arlington did. It is doubtful if any Englishman in the Resistance movement had as many narrow escapes from capture as Len and he was one of the very few people to get away from 'Captain Jack Evans'. He endured as much physical hardship — short of torture by the Nazis — as any Englishman who escaped from the Germans and stayed at large. Of course, in 1944 he did not know all this — but had he done so he would not have mentioned it. He was that sort of man.

Because Len's American uniform had no insignia of any kind he was frequently stopped in London by MPs; he would say loudly 'War Office' and produce his document stating that he was a repatriated escaped POW. This left the MPs speechless and Len enjoyed that.

He was in no mood for bureaucracy and especially the kind he encountered at the Army Pay Office in Knightsbridge, London. The paymaster lieutenant handed him back-pay of

£500, saying, 'I bet that makes you a very happy man.' He pushed Len a ledger. 'If you will just sign this. . . .'

Len pushed it straight back. 'I think you have forgotten something.'

'What could I possibly have forgotten?' the officer said, more surprised than irritated.

'This five hundred quid represents four and a half years' active service behind enemy lines, yes?' Len said.

'Yes, of course.'

'But during that time the army did not have to pay a penny towards my subsistence and not a penny towards my rations, as French civilians kept me supplied. That should entitle me to four and a half years' ration allowance.'

'Well, I'm damned!' the officer said. 'This really beats the lot! You are the first prisoner of war to come in here claiming ration allowance.'

Len said, 'That's just the point. I was *not* a prisoner of war. I was on active service.'

He explained to the confused and uncertain officer that he was not out to make a profit for himself, but French families who had risked their lives were entitled to some compensation from the British. In detail he told the paymaster about the Faucomprez family and what they had endured. In fact, Len had intended to give half his back-pay to Pierre but he knew it would never be accepted. 'It's a very strange case,' the officer said, 'but leave the family's name and address and I'll see what I can do.' And he meant it. Within weeks Pierre received the first cheque ever made out in his name – £70 from the British Army. At the time he was working fourteen hours a day for farmers and being paid the equivalent of thirty shillings (150p) a week. He went out that day and bought his first-ever brand new bicycle.

Len dealt with other frustrations in the way of a young old-soldier who had survived by his wits and his will for four and a half years. With other escaped prisoners and wounded soldiers out of convalescence homes, he was sent to Leeds on what the army called a 'Battle Training Course.' This meant long periods of drill and square bashing. All these men had six small red

stripes on their sleeves – one for each year of war service. The
corporal instructor had one. 'Right,' he said. 'You lot will forget
what you have just been through. As far as I am concerned you
are just another bunch of rookies.'

This approach did not appeal to the 'bunch of rookies'. Many
produced medical chits excusing them from marching. The
twenty who were left, perhaps with Len Arlington's incitement,
gave the bullying corporal the 'dumb soldier' treatment. When
he had them marching away from him they had him nailed, for
they knew from experience that when they reached the
extreme limit of the parade ground he would bellow 'About
turn!' And he did. But the men continued marching, then they
broke into double march, past the guardhouse and down the
street. The corporal caught up with them 500 yards away.

The RSM had observed this episode and, very angry, took
over from the corporal. When he gave them parade ground drill
the veterans gave him the 'open flower' treatment; that is, when
he ordered 'Right turn!' the men did many different things. A
couple kept marching on, a few did an about turn, some turned
left, two marked time on the spot . . . It was very satisfying to
see the RSM foaming at the mouth in impotent fury.

After many dreary months, Len volunteered for a posting to
Belgium or France – for obvious reasons. Instead he was sent to
Berlin, nearly a thousand miles from Lille. Posted to a car
company, he became in effect an army taxi driver. His very first
job was to pick up a German girl at eleven p.m. from British
Army HQ and drive her into the Russian zone and drop her
where she requested – all without asking questions.

Seeking an interview with a welfare officer, Len had difficulty
in finding the address in a city still without many street names.
He spotted an MP directing traffic and asked for directions.
The man stood a full minute, looking down at his boots
and scratching his head in deep concentration. Len recognised
these mannerisms. 'Freddie Fords, you old bastard!' he shouted.
This was his school pal, who had turned up at the barracks
in Guildford, again in France in 1940 and now, in December
1945, in Berlin.

That month Len was posted to a petrol company in Antwerp and it was from here that he put into effect plans to marry Marcelle. Bureaucracy reared its ugly head again. Although he was due to be demobilised in the following April, he was told by his CO that he needed special permission from the Commander in Chief himself to get married. 'This will take time,' he said. 'All I can advise is that you sign on for a further spell in the army.'

Under his breath Len said something rude. He had arranged for the marriage to take place in Chemy on March 23, 1946 and with only three days to go he had not found a way out. He had been finding solutions for nearly five years and here he was without one for the most important event of his life. Sitting troubled in his billet he overheard a comrade moaning about his bad luck on being detailed for guard duty, just when he had a date with his Belgian girlfriend. 'Which guard duty?' Len said absently.

'The bloody company offices!' his mate said. 'There's bugger-all to do, just sit all night in the company commander's office and make sure that nobody breaks in. . . .' At this point Len was acutely interested.

'Tell you what, mate,' he said generously. 'I'll help you out. I'll do that duty for you.'

'Blimey! You will?'

'For just a small favour. At Saturday morning's roll call you answer for me. I want to be somewhere else.'

Locked into the company commander's office by the orderly sergeant, Len got busy with the office stationery and equipment and with many false starts and revisions he tapped out on an imposing piece of offical letterhead an important message for the mayor of Chemy.

HEADQUARTERS BRITISH ARMY OF THE RHINE

I, General Shorebanks, Commanding Officer of the Rhine, authorise the marriage between Driver Leonard Arlington, 3rd Petroleum Company, BAOR and Mademoiselle Marcelle Faucomprez, French citizen of Chemy, France.

He spent two hours practising a likely signature and then he embellished the document with several circular rubber stamps. Len was pleased with the final appearance of his document, which he put in an envelope addressed to Monsieur le Maire, Chemy, Nord France. He had only one interruption that night. The telephone rang and, thinking the orderly sergeant might be calling to check that he had not gone to sleep, Len answered it.

'Yes,' he said, 'what the hell do you want?'

After a brief pause an angry voice demanded, 'Don't you usually address an officer as sir!'

Len said reasonably, 'How do I know you're an officer over the telephone?'

After a longer pause the caller hung up. 'Silly blighter,' Len said and went back to admiring his creative work.

Later that day he sent the document to Chemy by registered post. That Friday evening he set off, absent without leave, for Chemy and at two a.m. on Saturday morning reached Lille, where Pierre and Marcelle were waiting for him in the taxi owned by M. Dhenin of Gondecourt.

As he left the station building two prostitutes accosted him. 'Hullo, soldier,' one of them said in honeyed tones. 'Are you looking for something nice?'

'Come with us and have a night you will never forget,' the other said and her tongue twitching between bright red lips emphasised the offer.

'Have a heart, girls,' Len said cheerfuly. 'Tomorrow I'm getting married.'

The pair laughed, gave him a thumbs-up and made some ribald comments.

For another night Len had no sleep because the family sat up all night talking, until the time came to leave for the town hall. All was in order, Len was told; the certificate from the general had arrived. He had the feeling that the mayor and priest were impressed by his apparent close relationship with the Commander-in-Chief. The ceremony was quiet, with few guests, and those few from the Resistance, but it was still a long day of talking and feasting.

Len and Marcelle were to spend their wedding night in Auntie Marianne's house and they had hardly arrived in their bedroom, at one a.m., when all the guests, plus other people, arrived underneath their window. They sang until four a.m.

The newly married couple – the young soldier who had no idea that he had been heroic and the younger girl who had been through so much for him – were asleep soon after the revellers left. This time Len had no need for a rifle under his hand. This time he did not leave the cover off the skylight for a quick getaway. This time he did not wake up, with pounding heart, as the village dogs barked. He was at peace now.

17

AND AFTER

Len had difficulty in getting Marcelle across the frontier to Antwerp because he was travelling on a troop train with just one carriage, the last one, for civilians. Len was not prepared to allow his eighteen-year-old new wife to travel separately so he disguised her in his army overcoat and beret. Then, with the eager help of some soldiers from the Jewish Brigade serving with the British Army, he 'lost' her in a compartment of sprawling and sleeping khaki-clad figures. Whenever an official seemed about to make trouble on the protracted journey the Jewish Brigade men threatened him with all kinds of painful retribution. A few weeks after this, Marcelle received her brand-new passport as a British citizen.

Len Arlington returned to France in 1946 and worked there as a paint salesman until 1959. On his rounds he made a point of visiting all but one of the many people he had met during his escape from the Germans and while he was a Resistance fighter in occupied France. The one exception was the tobacco farmer and black marketeer Lestoquoi, for whom Len had no respect.

He returned to London to live in 1959 and in 1960 started work as a driver for Phillips Electrics Ltd.

His attachment to the many people who had helped him to elude the Germans remained strong. He could never fully understand why they had been prepared to risk so much for him and when, in later years, he asked them for an explanation, they gave him a deprecating shrug of the shoulders and a self-conscious smile and said, 'You took the greater risk, Lee-on-ar'.'

Marcelle also worked for Phillips, though with Len and her daughter Jenny, born on February 5, 1948, she often visited her parents and friends. In due course she presented her parents with three grandsons.

For his war service Len automatically qualified for certain British campaign medals – 1939–45 Star, War Medal, Defence Medal and France & Germany Star.

He received no British decoration but the French considered him a hero and awarded him the following: Croix du Combattant Résistance Volontaire; Crois du Combattant; Médaille d'Europe 1939–45; Confédération Européanne Ancien. The Reistance movement itself awarded him the Croix du Capitaine Michel, which was struck to honour Michael Trotobas of Len's own regiment. Belgium awarded him the Order of Leopold.

Marcelle was awarded the Croix du Combattant; Médaille Déportation, Internement et Résistance; Combattant Résistance Volontaire. She also won the Belgian Order of Leopold. Britain gave her the Deputy Supreme Commander's Certificate 'as a token of gratitude for and appreciation of the help given to Sailors, Soldiers and Airmen of the British Commonwealth of Nations, which enabled them to escape from, or evade capture by the enemy.' It was signed by Air Chief Marshal Tedder (later Lord Tedder).

Sophie (Fi-Fi) Faucomprez and her other daughter, Jervaise, received the same decorations as Marcelle except the Belgian Order of Leopold. They too received the Deputy Supreme Commander's certificate. Jervaise married and went to live in Sainghin, in the same district as Chemy.

Pierre Faucomprez had won the Croix de Guerre and Médaille Militaire in World War I. For his service in World War II he received the Médaille Déportation, Internement et Résistance; Croix du Combattant; Croix du Ancien Combattant. Later he received the highest French award, the Légion d'Honneur.

Florentine and Marie-Sophie Dhenin of the farming family who had been so helpful to Len and to the Resistance movement did not fare well in after years. Florentine lost her reason and left Gondecourt to live in a dirty two-room cottage in Allennes-les-Marais. Len visited her there and was appalled. The place had no heating or lighting and Florentine slept on a wooden table without covering. Len took up her case with the mayor of Gondecourt and reminded him of the murdered German sergeant. The mayor said that as Florentine no longer lived in his town nothing could be done for her. Len spoke to the mayor of Allennes-les-Marais, who said that as she was not a native of his town he was unable to help her. Len did what he could. Marie-Sophie stayed on her farm – the one from which George Young had made such a spectacular crash-diving escape – with her son Paul. Paul became a local celebrity when it was known after the war that it was he who had found the dead German in his farm field. In Marie-Sophie's old age her greatest pleasure was a visit from Len Arlington. 'Ah, Lee-on-ar',' she would say. 'La guerre!' When I looked at this frail woman I wondered where she found the strength to carry the corpse of the big German. She died soon after Len and I had visited her in September 1982.

Fate dealt harshly with Joseph and Lucienne Wiplier, that brave and cheerful couple to whom Len owed so much, and their family. Lucienne died of cirrhosis of the liver, though she was a teetotaller, in 1962. Joseph had a minor accident but gangrené set in and he died in 1963. Jo-Jo, deeply depressed by business reverses, committed suicide and his brother Henri, who had suffered for six months in the Nazi penal camp for the Annoeullin miners, died of a heart attack on his daughter's twenty-first birthday, on January 1, 1971. Only Lucette, who had given Len his chocolate ration, survived.

Marcel Fertein, much-decorated, went back to the business of making window shutters. A quiet and sensitive man, he had revered Michael Trotobas and he often said that his best days were those he spent with that 'dynamic' British officer while fighting agains the Nazis. For many years he made the major speech each year at the Trotobas commemorative ceremonies in Lille.

Felicien Lemaire returned from Buchenwald concentration camp so broken in health that he had to be carried into his home. He and Len never again spoke of the 'Captain Jack incident' or of the death of his son, Ernest. He lived in pain and died prematurely as a result of his suffering.

Most of the many people of the Lille-Gondecourt-Lens-Seclin region who helped Len Arlington were considerably older than he was and one by one they died, several at all too young an age. René Saublin died soon after the war, his death probably hastened by the injuries he suffered in the wartime road accident. Zelfa Ringot, a key figure in wartime Gondecourt, was another who died prematurely, in 1948. In the 1980s her sons Edouard and Jean-Marie were the only Ringots still living. Edouard occasionally chided Len Arlington for getting him drunk in 1941. The only adult friend of Len's to move right away from the Lille area was Marcelle Brien, the expert in false identities, who married an Australian and went to live in Australia.

George Young, Grenadier Guards, and Len Wilson, Middlesex Regiment, reached Marseilles after leaving Gondecourt. Young disappeared one night and no trace of him was ever found. Wilson stowed away on a ship leaving for North Africa, but was discovered and imprisoned on arrival. The Vichy French put him on trial for spying and he was condemned to death. The Allied invasion of North Africa in the summer of 1943 saved his life. Returned to Britain, Wilson was invalided out of the army.

Jack Farnell vanished from Len's life but Len was confident that he would prosper; Farnell was a natural survivor.

Bill Jackson ('Jack') and Stan Golding, after their capture in Haisnes and imprisonment in the infamous Gestapo cells of Arras, were sent to a prisoner-of-war camp and were later transferred to other camps. After the Arras prison the ordinary camps were bearable enough. On the day Jack was put into the Arras cell he had scratched a calendar on his wall so that he could keep track of time; he believed that if he could remain time-orientated the Gestapo would not be so easily able to break him. In later years Jack and Stan both suffered from remorse over the deaths of their French friends and when they met Len Arlington in 1979 – for the first time since 1942 – they wept in recollection. Neither of the men ever returned to France and this disappointed those French people who had helped them and who survived.

The Broukes – brother and sister – who had given Len a job on their farm after he had escaped from the Germans and was on the run in 1940 became known as Nazi collaborators but escaped punishment after the war for reasons nobody can explain. In 1947 Len called on Mr Brouke and asked him why he had helped him in 1940, considering that his sympathies lay with the Germans. Brouke said, 'Quite honestly, I have been asking myself that question ever since.'

My guess is that he was disarmed by Len's cheerful nature – and by his willingness to do a hard day's work.

Henriette Verbeke, who had betrayed Madame Passy, was tried in 1946 and sentenced to life; she actually served about ten years. Marcelle Faucomprez (Mrs Arlington) was not called as a witness but the message she had relayed from the condemned Madame Passy was damning evidence against Mme Verbeke.

'Joe', the German agent who had posed as a British officer, was sighted in the town of Carvin in 1946 when he returned to visit people he had known. He was told that Len Arlington was living in the district and quickly left, never to be heard of again.

Alex Keiller was seen, in uniform and at large, in Loos prison, Lille. In fact he was there because the Nazis considered the place was safe for him, but a Resistance man in the gaol told him that if he did not get out his throat would be cut. He disappeared but years later, for no apparent reason, he sent Len a postcard from Gibraltar. British and French investigators never did catch up with him.

Mathilde-Lily Carré, 'the Cat', was charged with treason; she was forty-one when her trial began on January 3, 1949. A total of thirty-three witnesses gave evidence again her, but as the prosecutor said there were many 'silent witnesses' – the people she had betrayed. She had been known as 'the Cat' among her comrades when she was a genuine Resistance worker and the label was then an affectionate one. When she went over to the Nazis it became notorious. She was sentenced to death but was reprieved because she had, after all, later become a triple agent working once again for the Allies. Her sentence was commuted to twenty years' hard labour. Because of ill health she was

released on September 7, 1954. Few of the men into whom
'the Cat' sank her claws survived; Len Arlington outplayed her
that winter's day in the Lemaire house in Annoeullin.

Captain Heinz Eckert (Captain Jack Evans) operated in several
regions. On one occasion, on the Brittany coast, while engaged in
a complex plot to get his spy Mathilde Carré picked up by the
Royal Navy and taken to London, he arrested two newly arrived
SOE agents and made a haul of two radio transmitters, 600,000
francs in notes, a file of forged French and German documents,
passes and identity cards, twenty-five Sten guns, other weapons
and much explosive. Later he did stage-manage the 'escape' of the
Cat to England and then became chief of a new Abwehr post at
Lyons. Eckert gathered around him a gang of cunning and ruthless
men and used them to hunt down Resistance leaders and SOE
agents. He personally infiltrated several réseaux in the guise of an
SOE officer and learnt that London was making persistent
inquiries about Dieppe. His reports led the Germans to strengthen
their defences around the port, with calamitous consequences for
the British-Canadian raid. Eckert watched this battle. He was
nearly always successful and trapped hundreds of Resistance men,
SOE agents and escapers. Len Arlington was one of the very few
people to outwit him.

Michael Trotobas, killed in November 1943, is the best known
Resistance name in northern France. His wartime réseau continued
into peacetime as Organisation Française Les Compagnons et Amis
du Capitaine Michael (OFACM), an association of Resistance
veterans who wished to perpetuate his memory and that of
comrades who had died while serving with his movement. Each
year, on the Sunday nearest the anniversary of his death,
ceremonies are held at No. 20 Boulevard de Belfort, at the
cemetery where he and other Resistance men are buried, and at
Lille Town Hall. After much solemn and moving ceremonial the
veterans then attend a reunion dinner.

OFACM cuts clean across the bitter divisions of French
politics and class. Among its members are Gaullists, militant
Communists, Christian Democrats, Socialists; there are miners,
artisans and labourers, wealthy industrialists, businessmen and

shopkeepers. Many of them hate what the others stand for but nearly all the 200 people who attend the reunion dinner have one thing in common: They were labelled 'terrorists and criminals' by the Nazis and many of them were in Nazi prisons. Bemedalled and highly decorated they reminisce at length about exploits which they would never tell outsiders. Those who knew Michael Trotobas personally or served with his Sylvestre Farmer *réseau* (also known as Buckmaster Sylvestre and War Office) wear the distinctive 'Croix du Capitaine Michel.' As an honorary member of the postwar association I too am privileged to wear this cross.

Unhappily, Britain never did adequately recognise the many French and Belgian people who helped British servicemen to evade capture or recapture. Perhaps this was because the British people as a whole did not understand the terrible dangers to which the French and Belgians deliberately exposed themselves when aiding Allied soldiers and airmen. Punishment was often exemplary – execution or deportation to a German concentration camp. The United States awarded the Medal of Freedom to those people who helped American servicemen. British awards were parsimoniously awarded and only a few people received them.

POSTSCRIPT

Len Arlington telephoned me one night in January 1983 to tell me, in great distress, that Clotaire Durot had died. Clotaire was the youth of seventeen with the mutilated shotgun with which he proposed to shoot at German soldiers, and in preventing him from doing so Len had saved his life. They became good friends after the war. On one occasion, at a Trotobas commemoration dinner, I sat between Len and Clotaire and many times intercepted the conversation that they had with their eyes; they were remembering the events of the war. Other friends of Len had died in the few months before the death of Clotaire and he was upset too by the failing health of his old *réseau* chief, Marcel Fertein. He and I had recently visited Marie-Sophie Dhenin, the gallant woman who had walked into a lions' den of German soldiers to rescue Young and Wilson. She, too, was fading. We talked about Clotaire and others for a long time that night but I remember one comment in particular which Len made. 'I hope that we all meet again somewhere, sometime.' They deserve to.

Len himself died at Hassocks, Sussex, in September 1994. He was 73. This might seem to be a 'fair age' but it is reasonable to believe that Len would have lived longer had he not been subjected to many privations during the war. Sleeping in the open during a continental winter must have taken its toll on his long-term health. I had seen him not long before his death and he had been his usual irrepressible Cockney self, but his war still loomed large in his memory. Until 1993 he and Marcelle had travelled to Lille in France for the annual commemoration of Resistance exploits and in particular those of the réseau that had been led by Michael Trotobas until he was killed by the Gestapo in November 1943.

Over the years following the publication of this book in 1984 various people wrote to me asking to be put in touch with Len Arlington. I always first checked these approaches with him and if they came from people in the Resistance Len was pleased to make contact with them.

But there were others. . . . One day I received a letter from a man in his forties who told me that his father, also a British Army evader of the Nazis, had joined the Resistance. He sent me a long obituary notice from a provincial newspaper which referred to his father as a hero of the Resistance who had been awarded the British Military Medal for his services. According to the report, he was generally known in Northern France as the Pimpernel. This former serviceman was now dead but his son was planning to take his mother 'on a trip down memory lane', as he expressed it. They would visit various places and people in the Lille region, people who no doubt would recall the 'Pimpernel'. To begin with, his son asked me, could I put him in touch with Len Arlington.

On a visit to Len I relayed this information. His features became frozen, his eyes sombre and his manner strange. 'Can you get me a photograph of this Pimpernel?' he asked. 'I mean, a wartime photograph.' He said no more at the time. A few weeks later I arrived with the requested photograph, obtained from the man's son. Len scrutinised it. 'Oh yes, I can arrange to see this man,' he said tautly.

'But as I told you,' I said, 'he is dead.'

'If he were alive I'd kill him,' this gentle man said. 'I would have to kill him.' And he meant it.

The supposed hero had in fact been a traitor who had betrayed British evaders and escapers as well as French Resistance men and women. I was with Len in France when he showed the photo to his former comrades and without exception they remembered the man with revulsion.

Having discussed the matter at some length, Len and I decided tactfully to seal off the past for the traitor's son. Len did not wish to meet him nor did he want him to be told the truth about his father. 'It's not the boy's fault,' he said, 'and we can't blame his mother. They can't be punished for what that bastard did.'

I explained to the younger man that Len no longer wanted to remember the war and that most of the people his father had known were dead. 'Memory Lane', I suggested, might depress his mother. I heard no more from him and I hope that he did not search northern France for his father's friends. They might not have been as kind as Len Arlington.

There have been better memories. In June 1996 I received a letter from Stewart Kent. It read: 'I have just finished reading your fascinating book and I was amazed to read for the first time the exploits of my grandmother, Mrs J. Pachy, and my mother Yvonne Pachy during the last war. They both knew and helped Len Arlington. I hope to meet Len's widow, who was the last person to see my grandmother alive in Loos prison. I have telephoned my mother in France and she was thrilled to hear of your book.'

In fact, Mr Kent's mother is pictured in the book with Michael Trotobas. The family name is, as shown in Mr Kent's letter, Pachy. Len Arlington always believed that the spelling was Passy.

With others, Yvonne Pachy and Marcelle Arlington were reunited a few months after I received Mr Kent's letter and, as Mr Kent later said, 'There was not a dry eye among them.' Of course, they spoke at length about Len Arlington and about the brave Jeanne Pachy, one of many French patriots murdered by the Nazis. On her memorial plaque in Gondecourt she is commemorated as Jeanne Oliger, her maiden name. Marcelle explained that, unlike Madame Pachy – executed by the Nazis – her parents, the defiant Pierre Faucomprez and his vivacious wife Fi-Fi, had lived to a good age and died peacefully.

Gallant people who live through great dangers and many tensions, relieved only by a reciprocal trust in one another and a common hatred of a vile enemy, are generally sentimental at a later meeting. Had Len Arlington lived to see Yvonne Pachy again he too would have been tearful.

From 1945 until his death Len's greatest pleasure was in meeting former comrades of the French Resistance and talking about their days of daring and defiance against overwhelming odds.

John Laffin